CLARENDON LIBRARY OF
LOGIC AND PHILOSOPHY

General Editor
L. JONATHAN COHEN
The Queen's College, Oxford

THE FORTUNES OF INQUIRY

'Truth, daughter of Time' (Imprint of the Marcolino Press, after a woodcut in
Adriaen Willaert, Cinque messe, Venice, 1536)

THE FORTUNES OF INQUIRY

❧

NICHOLAS JARDINE

CLARENDON PRESS · OXFORD
1986

Oxford University Press, Walton Street, Oxford OX2 6DP
Oxford New York Toronto
Delhi Bombay Calcutta Madras Karachi
Kuala Lumpur Singapore Hong Kong Tokyo
Nairobi Dar es Salaam Cape Town
Melbourne Auckland
and associated companies in
Beirut Berlin Ibadan Nicosia

Oxford is a trade mark of Oxford University Press

Published in the United States
by Oxford University Press, New York

British Library Cataloguing in Publication Data
Jardine, N.
The fortunes of inquiry.——(Clarendon
library of logic and philosophy)
1. Science——Philosophy
I. Title
501 Q175
ISBN 0-19-824929-2

Library of Congress Cataloging-in-Publication Data
Jardine, Nicholas.
The fortunes of inquiry.
(Clarendon library of logic and philosophy)
Includes index.
1. Science——Philosophy. 2. Science——Methodology.
3. Truth. I. Title. II. Series.
Q175.J346 1986 501 86-8698
ISBN 0-19-824929-2

Set by Wyvern Typesetting Ltd, Bristol
Printed in Great Britain
at the University Printing House, Oxford
by David Stanford
Printer to the University

FOR JENNY

Acknowledgements

My greatest intellectual debts are to the published works of Wilfrid Sellars, Hilary Putnam, Bernard Williams, and Mary Hesse. Whilst writing I profited in conversation from defences of tough-minded realist and relativist positions by, respectively, Dave Papineau and Simon Schaffer. I am indebted for telling comments on a draft of the work to Mary Hesse, Hugh Mellor, and a reader for Oxford University Press. I thank Adam Hodgkin, Angela Blackburn, and Hilary McGlynn for much help and encouragement.

Contents

I

Introduction

MY primary concern in this work is with the status and credentials of the claim that the natural sciences have shown an accumulation of truth. For reasons that will emerge in due course, I shall call this claim 'scientific absolutism'.

The most superficial chronicler of recent intellectual history could scarcely fail to record the spread of doubts and reservations about scientific absolutism. Nor is it just the more presumptuous forms of the doctrine—those which arrogate attainment of truth to the natural sciences alone or which see in their history an approach to a complete and unified science of nature—that are challenged. Even the more temperate forms—those which concede the limited, sporadic, and piecemeal nature of accumulation of truth in the sciences—are widely called in question.

It is customary in discussing the causes of loss of faith in the march of science to rehearse the oft-told tale of the collapse of logical positivism and of its 'successor' hypothetico-deductivism. In the same vein it might be argued that present doubts owe much to recent loss of confidence in scientific realism, in the last two decades widely used as a metaphysical underpinning for the view that the natural sciences have manifested a growth of objective knowledge. As explanations these are, I think, misguided in the weight they attach to developments within the philosophy of science. Unsurprisingly, given that it is manifestly a historical thesis that is at issue, it is above all in the historiography of science that the origins of disillusion with it are to be found, origins which greatly antedate the recent philosophical onslaught on positivism.[1]

Linear accumulation of knowledge and the autonomy of the mathematical and experimental sciences have been dominant

---

[1] Due emphasis on the historiographical roots of current crises in the philosophy of science is to be found in M. B. Hesse, *Revolutions and Reconstructions in the Philosophy of Science*, Brighton, 1980.

historiographical themes from the early nineteenth century, the time of proliferation of 'heroic' narrations of achievement in the sciences, to the establishment of history of science as an academically institutionalized discipline in the 1920s and 30s.[2] However, this orthodoxy has never entirely prevailed. Thus early nineteenth-century histories of the sciences quite often use a scheme of epochs of development punctuated by major innovations, transformations, or revolutions.[3] In the majority of such epochal histories the overall theme is one of progress mediated by adherence to proper methods; but in a substantial minority we find motifs of Romantic historiography, the epochs of the sciences being described in terms of organic transformation and differentiation rather than linear progress, in terms of the spiritual expressions of peoples and cultures rather than exercise of reason and method.[4] Later in the century, with the growth of critical scholarship in the historiography of science, we may detect increased realization that the history of the sciences cannot be divorced either from the history of philosophy and theology or from the history of folk beliefs and practices. A generation on in the works of Ernst Cassirer, Emile Meyerson, Edwin Burtt, and Arthur Lovejoy there is major emphasis on the inextricability of the history of the natural sciences from the history of the 'metaphysical' doctrines and systems that empiricist and positivist epistemology had long sought to oust. In these authors the autonomy and linearity of scientific development are variously called in question; but it is in the writings of Alexandre Koyré that the challenge to prevailing modes of historiography of science

---

[2] On the history of historiography of science see A. Thackray, 'History of science', in P. T. Durbin, ed., *A Guide to the Culture of Science, Technology and Medicine*, New York, 1980, 3–69; 'The pre-history of an academic discipline: the study of the history of science in the United States, 1891–1941', *Minerva*, 18 (1980), 448–73. On the history of medical historiography see E. Heischkel, 'Die Geschichte der Medizingeschichtschreibung', in W. Artelt, ed., *Einführung in die Medizinhistorik*, Stuttgart, 1949, pp. 203–37.

[3] The notable English example of epochal historiography of science is William Whewell's *History of the Inductive Sciences*, 3 vols., London, 1837. On revolution as a theme in early nineteenth-century historiography of science see W. Lepenies, *Das Ende der Naturgeschichte. Wandel kultureller Selbstverstandlichkeiten in den Wissenschaften des 18. und 19. Jahrhunderts*, Munich, 1976, p. 106 ff.

[4] On historiography of science in the Romantic period see, e.g., Lepenies, op. cit.; H. von Seemen, *Zur Kenntnis der Medizinhistorie in der deutschen Romantik*, Zurich, 1926.

becomes most fully apparent.[5] Koyré's masterpieces concentrate on the metaphysical and cosmological discontinuities that have marked the history of scientific thought, and they highlight the extent to which not only the first-order contents of the sciences but also ideals of scientific explanation and procedure have been subject to drastic mutation.

Koyré's approach poses also a more specific threat to positivist historiography. In his essays on Galilean science he repeatedly emphasizes the extent to which the data of mathematical science are constituted not by raw untutored experience, but by experience selected and interpreted in the light of theory. In the writings of two near contemporaries of Koyré, Gaston Bachelard and Ludwik Fleck, the positivist conception of a fixed realm of fact, ever more completely described and systematized with the advance of science, is effectively challenged on rather different historiographical grounds. Bachelard is concerned to show how far removed are the phenomena in which mathematical science is grounded, the quantified constructs of the laboratory, from 'common' experience variously distorted by pre-scientific obsessions.[6] Ludwik Fleck, in perhaps the most profoundly innovative single work in twentieth-century history of science, argues that there has been a multiplicity of incommensurable 'thought-styles' that direct and constrain all scientific activity, including observation and experiment; and he offers a series of hypotheses about the individual and group psychological processes that mediate the establishment of novel facts in the context of a thought-style.[7] It is, however, Thomas Kuhn's masterly synthesis of these diverse lines of attack that has come to epitomize the revolt against linear cumulative historiography.[8]

[5] On the magnitude of Koyré's impact on recent historiography of science see, for example, T. S. Kuhn, 'Alexandre Koyré and the history of science. On an intellectual revolution', *Encounter*, 34 (1970), 67–9, and C. C. Gillispie, 'Koyré, Alexandre', *Dictionary of Scientific Biography*, 7 (1973), 482–90. A list of his works is in *Mélanges Alexandre Koyré*, vol. 1, Paris, 1973.

[6] See especially, G. Bachelard, *Le nouvel esprit scientifique*, Paris, 1934, and *La formation de l'esprit scientifique*, Paris, 1938. Interesting accounts of this aspect of Bachelard's thought are given by S. Gaukroger, 'Bachelard and the problem of epistemological analysis', *Studies in History and Philosophy of Science*, 7 (1976), 189–244, pp. 212–23, and S. Schaffer, 'Natural philosophy', in G. S. Rousseau and R. Porter, eds., *The Ferment of Knowledge*, Cambridge, 1980, 55–91, pp. 74–84.

[7] L. Fleck, *Entstehung und Entwicklung einer wissenschaftlichen Tatsache* [1935]; trans. F. Bradley and T. J. Trenn, *Genesis and Development of a Scientific Fact*, Chicago, 1979.

[8] T. S. Kuhn, *The Structure of Scientific Revolutions*, Chicago, 1962.

The quite dramatic turning away from this style of history writing that has occurred in the past decade reflects not only the influence of Kuhn and his intellectual sources within the discipline, but also certain more general shifts of historiographic interest and presupposition. Two of these have substantial implications for the present work.

In the heyday of cumulative and retrospective history writing it was common practice to present the history of science as if all the antecedents of present-day science were products of a single vast enterprise stretching back to the philosopher-priests of Babylonia and Egypt or the cosmological speculators of Ionia. Many factors have conspired to undermine this simplistic view. Study and appreciation of classical Chinese science and technology and of medieval Arabic science have made it plain that even the narrowest focus on contributions to 'positive knowledge' cannot confine the history of science to a single cultural tradition. The recent proliferation of studies of early modern European history of science has made it abundantly clear that the now dominant tradition of mathematical-cum-experimental science emerged from the interactions of a plurality of disciplines and traditions of inquiry, many of them not in any strict modern sense scientific. Yet further appreciation of the sheer diversity of types and traditions of inquiry into nature is beginning to accrue from the growth of social and institutional history of science. In this field it is widely held that many crucial historical and sociological issues concerning the development of science are best addressed without undue regard for the question whether particular past scientific beliefs did or did not anticipate current beliefs or whether particular past traditions of inquiry were or were not directly implicated in the genesis of our science.[9]

A second recent shift in historiographic presupposition that will concern us has to do with interpretation. In an influential paper Quentin Skinner has documented ways in which historians of ideas have been wont, through failure to appreciate the distance between past cognitive standpoints and their own, to attribute to past

---

[9] For a list of recent studies that pay at least lip-service to this symmetry principle see B. Barnes and D. Bloor, 'Relativism, rationalism and the sociology of knowledge', in M. Hollis and S. Lukes, eds., *Rationality and Relativism*, Oxford, 1982, 21–47, n.9.

authors meanings they could not possibly have intended.[10] Skinner calls these sources of systematic distortion 'mythologies': there is, for example, the 'mythology of doctrines' according to which it is assumed that past authors were addressing questions in the ranges that the historian takes to be constitutive of the disciplines to which he assigns their works; there is the 'mythology of prolepsis' in the grip of which the historian seeks out and emphasizes whatever in past authors can be made to appear to conform with or adumbrate current beliefs; and there is the 'mythology of parochialism', which leads the historian to interpretations that create specious familiarity in the works of past authors through the uncritical use of present-day categories. The past decade has shown a greatly enhanced awareness amongst historians of science that reading of primary sources is a risky business; and it is now widely appreciated that even the most accessible and amenable texts cannot safely be regarded as unproblematic registers of scientific beliefs and the reasons that sustained them. Such hermeneutic awareness is surely a precondition of escape from the mythologies that Skinner so engagingly parades. Certainly there is ample evidence in recent historiography of science of increased sensitivity to the dangers of anachronism. In particular, the uncritical use of present-day technical terminology and notation in translation and exegesis is on the wane. There is evidence too of greater wariness of the pitfalls in exegesis and explication of primary sources that arise from the gulfs between past and present disciplines, methods of inquiry, genres, and rhetorical and dialectical conventions.

Post-Koyréan historiography of science has raised serious objections to many of the stronger versions of scientific absolutism. In the course of this work I shall endorse a number of those objections. Thus, it will be agreed that scientific development has been mediated by a multiplicity of traditions of inquiry; that there is no fixed agenda of scientific questions, but rather a turnover of questions, old questions being dissolved and new questions generated by new theories and new styles of inquiry; that the history of science has not evinced a steady accumulation of truth; that scientific progress has not come about through adherence by inquirers to any universally

---

[10] Q. Skinner, 'Meaning and understanding in the history of ideas', *History and Theory*, 8 (1969), 3–53. On the debates surrounding and occasioned by Skinner's critique see D. Boucher, *Texts in Context. Revisionist Methods for Studying the History of Ideas*, The Hague, 1985.

applicable canon of scientific method; and that the history of science is at odds with a view of scientific inquiry as tending towards a complete and unified science of nature.

Despite this agreement with central tenets of the new historiography of science, certain of the philosophical conclusions that have been drawn from it will be resisted. Claims about the existence of radical discontinuities in the history of the sciences have been widely held to be conducive to a relativization of truth to paradigm or conceptual scheme. Similarly, claims about the diversity of methods of inquiry and justification that have prevailed at various times in various disciplines have sometimes been held to warrant relativization of truth in science to methodology or style of inquiry. Others have found in the history of science grounds not for relativism about truth, but rather for indictment of the whole project of constructing a philosophical theory of truth. In this work neither relativism about truth nor abandonment of truth as a subject of philosophical reflection will emerge as warranted reactions to discontinuity of content and diversity of style of inquiry in the history of science.

The account of truth in science to be offered here is premised on an outright rejection of realist accounts of truth as correspondence to a mind-independent 'real world'.[11] In addition to scientific absolutism itself, however, a considerable number of further claims customarily associated with scientific realism will be at least tacitly endorsed. We shall, for example, accept the basic scientific realist claim that by and large the notions of truth and falsity are applicable to the components of scientific theories taken at face value—across the board from fundamental postulates to experimental laws, auxiliary hypotheses, and boundary conditions. We shall tacitly accept too the view that acquisition of true beliefs is a primary aim of scientific inquiry and that the technological progress of the past four or so centuries is in part to be explained by its success in achieving that aim. Yet further realist doctrines will either be indirectly endorsed, being treated as well-confirmed scientific hypotheses, or countenanced, being treated as open scientific issues. To these

[11] M. Devitt, *Realism and Truth*, Oxford, 1984, ch. 4, argues cogently against supposed connections between accounts of truth as correspondence to a mind-independent world and theses of common-sense and scientific realism. However, the weight of established usage makes it hard to follow Devitt in refusing to describe such accounts of truth as realist. In the following pages I have characterized accounts of truth as correspondence to the world as 'metaphysical realist'.

categories belong 'common-sense' realist claims to the effect that the universe could exist devoid of minds, indeed probably has done so and may well do so again, and that the majority of the constituents of the universe are in no sense causal products of our mental processes.[12] Here too belong what have been called 'the causal ingredients' of scientific realism, claims about the explicability of our acquisition of true perceptual and theoretical beliefs in terms of reliable causal processes originating in the objects of those beliefs and mediated by our senses.

I have indicated above some of the many ways in which general theses about the nature of science and scientific inquiry have proved vulnerable to developments in the historiography of science. It was reflection on the extent of this vulnerability that suggested the basic strategy of this work, that of attempting to secularize metaphysical claims about science by construing them as hypotheses about the fortunes of scientific inquiry. The framework for this programme of historical assimilation is provided by an account of truth in terms of the eventual verdicts of inquiries which satisfy certain stringent conditions. On this account truth is entirely independent of the natures and standpoints of inquirers. Such independence has been presented by Bernard Williams as the mark of an 'absolute' conception of the world, and it is in this sense that the term is used in characterizing as scientific absolutism the claim that the sciences have shown an accumulation of truth.[13]

This work professes pragmatist sympathies, notably in its chariness of metaphysical notions that resist naturalistic or historical reconstrual and in its concern to ground truth and rationality in the processes and fortunes of inquiry. Its pragmatism is, however, atypical in crucial respects. Thus it is at odds with the classical forms of pragmatism in its refusal to subordinate truth to method or rationality; yet it diverges sharply from certain later manifestations of pragmatism in the conceptual distance it maintains between truth and currently attainable consensus. In terms of the all-too-fluid current taxonomy of philosophical stances, the position I shall defend is perhaps a species of 'internal' realism. Certainly it shares

---

[12] These and other claims associated with the notion of 'mind-independence' of the world are interestingly discussed by G. Hellman, 'Realist principles', *Philosophy of Science*, 50 (1983), 227–49.

[13] B. A. O. Williams, *Descartes: the Project of Pure Enquiry*, Harmondsworth, 1978, chs. 2 and 10; 'The scientific and the ethical', in S. C. Brown, ed., *Objectivity and Cultural Divergence*, Cambridge, 1984, pp. 209–28.

a number of assumptions and prejudices with Putnam's internal realism, which purports to sustain a range of common-sensical realist theses together with a rejection of relativism without commitment to an account of truth as correspondence to a mind-independent world or to the existence of a universally valid canon of scientific rationality.[14] It is, however, thoroughly misleading to call this kind of account 'internal' or 'immanent', for that carries the implication that there is an 'external' or 'transcendent' standpoint from which the realist theses might be seen not to hold. The philosophical position at issue denies not only the attainability of such an external standpoint, but also the intelligibility of the very notion of such a standpoint.[15]

In the following pages I shall reject and try to move beyond both metaphysical realist and relativist doctrines concerning truth in the sciences. However, only a modest parade of largely unoriginal criticisms of the rejected doctrines will be mounted. What originality there is in this attempt to 'overcome' metaphysical realism and relativism lies not in direct attack, but rather in showing how a pragmatic account of truth can capture both common-sense realist claims of the sorts mentioned above and the common-sense claims about conceptual and methodological diversity that lend credence to relativism.

The plan of the work is as follows. In Chapter II a pragmatic account of truth as the limit of inquiry is outlined and criticized for its failure to do justice either to truth's transcendence of error and limitation or to its immanence in history. Acting on morals drawn from the limit-of-inquiry account, I offer in Chapter III an account of truth in terms of the eventual verdicts of inquiries which satisfy powerful coherence conditions. The conditions have to do with the capacity of an inquiry to resolve questions, to recognize and overcome sources of error, and to explain divergences between its own deliverances and those of other inquiries. Subsequent chapters are concerned with promotion and defence of scientific absolutism in the context of this pragmatic account of truth.

The basic argument for scientific absolutism is set out in Chapter

---

[14] H. Putnam, 'Realism and reason', in *Meaning and the Moral Sciences*, London, 1978, 123–40; *Reason, Truth and History*, Cambridge, 1982; 'Why there isn't a ready-made world', *Synthese*, 51 (1982), 141–67.

[15] Perhaps 'quasi-realism' is a more appropriate term: cf. S. Blackburn, 'Truth, realism and the regulation of theory', *Midwest Studies in Philosophy*, 5 (1980), 353–71.

IV. The core of the argument is an inductive extrapolation from aspects of the history of science to hypotheses about the fortunes of scientific inquiry indefinitely protracted under favourable circumstances. The hypotheses are to the effect that such an inquiry would encounter no irresoluble general questions, no insuperable sources of error, and no inexplicably divergent outcomes of alien inquiries. The historical argument for scientific absolutism requires fortification against two main types of objections. First there are those that would undermine the interpretations of the history of science on which the argument is premissed. The theses of incommensurability of rival theories and indeterminacy of intertheoretic interpretation provide bases for objections of this type, and in Chapter V I attempt to counter them. A second type of objection arises from philosophical theses that directly threaten the hypotheses about the fortunes of an indefinitely prolonged scientific inquiry on which the case for scientific absolutism rests. Every one of those hypotheses is menaced by the thesis of underdetermination of theory by data. In Chapter VI I attempt to fend off this menace. In so doing, however, strong claims are made about the availability of reliable methods for the resolution of theoretical conflict. Chapters VII and VIII are concerned with ways in which these claims may be substantiated: the former deals with 'surface justification', the establishment of reliability of methods through calibration against standards and precedents; the latter deals with 'deep justification', causal explanation of the reliability of methods. Chapter IX completes the defence of scientific absolutism by considering the credentials and consequences of certain theses about the existence of insuperable limits to scientific inquiry. In the final chapter I review some of the philosophical commitments incurred in the course of the work and contrast them to commitments incurred by realist defences of scientific absolutism. The chapter concludes with mention of outstanding questions concerning the mode of accumulation of truth in the sciences and the viability of absolutism in other domains of inquiry.

II

Standards for Truth

TRUTH is a notion with rich metaphysical connotations. Central to the present work is the thought that truth is absolutely uncontaminated with error and entirely unconditioned by the standpoint of any particular inquirer or type of inquirers. The absolute and unconditioned nature of truth has often been associated with its transcendence of human cognitive capacities. On the one hand it may be held that truth is such that our grasp of it is inevitably insecure. Such claims range from humdrum fallibilism, the claim that few, if any, of our beliefs are certain, to the striking claim that all our beliefs may be false—may be delusions inculcated by a malicious demon or his descendant, the malevolent neurophysiologist. On the other hand truth may be held to be such that our grasp of it is inevitably incomplete. Such claims for the elusiveness of truth range from the modest view that there will always be as yet undiscovered truths to the claim that there may be truths that are utterly inaccessible to all conceivable types of inquirers.

The pragmatic account of truth to be offered in the next chapter is premissed on the view that epistemic insecurity and elusiveness are not primitive but derivative features of truth, derivative, that is, from the basic premiss that truth transcends all sources of error and all partial perspectives together with the assumption, suggested by reflection on the biologically and socially conditioned nature of our inquiries and well attested by the history of science, that the outcomes of human inquiry are on many counts prone to error and partiality. The account is inconsistent with a certain extreme version of the epistemic elusiveness thesis, a version which maintains that there may be truths that are beyond the reach of all conceivable types of inquiry. It is, however, compatible with the claim that there may be truths forever beyond our grasp. Further, it is consistent with strong claims about the fallibility of our beliefs, both singly and severally.

There is another, and historically prior, cluster of connotations associated with the notion that truth functions as an absolute measure, standard, or bench-mark for all claims to knowledge. Here belong various views of truth as completely determinate, indivisible, homogeneous, and immutable. Neither the intelligibility nor the plausibility of such ontological images of truth is directly discussed in this work; but the final chapter includes reflections distinctly inhospitable to the idea that the truth attained by science is describable, however metaphorically, in such terms.

It is surely no accident that with the demise of positivism there has been an epidemic of realist metaphysics in the ranks of philosophers of science. For despite their great disparity in content the positivist and scientific realist ideologies are at one in crediting the natural sciences with a special relationship to reality. For positivists the natural sciences have a prerogative as vehicles of positive knowledge, by virtue of their special relationship to the experiential foundations of knowledge. From Condillac to Carnap this assumption remained intact despite extraordinary vicissitudes in positivist conceptions of the nature of the experiential foundation, of the relation to it that is prerequisite for full cognitive respectability, and of the proper attitude to disciplines whose deliverances fail positivist tests of cognitive significance. For scientific realists the natural sciences have a prerogative as potential bearers of objective truth by virtue of their having as their manifest subject-matter 'the world', the ultimate arbiter of truth. Here again a respectful, if not obsequious, attitude to the natural sciences is a constant factor amidst a bewildering variety of views about the contents and structures of the world, about the nature of the correspondence with that world which constitutes truth, and about the proper attitude to disciplines whose subject matters are related either indirectly or not at all to the world.

As I emphasized in the Introduction, doctrines associated with scientific realism will be endorsed in the course of this book. But these scientific realist doctrines will be defended in the context of an outright rejection of the view that truth can be explicated in terms of correspondence, isomorphism, or conformity with the world. I believe the standard and long-standing objection to such correspondence theories of truth to be conclusive. Truth cannot be explicated as a relation of correspondence between beliefs and the world, because we can form no substantive conception of such a relation.

The recent history of philosophy amply attests, alas, to the inefficacy of the objection. In the hope of dispelling this most resilient of metaphysical illusions a variety of analytical tactics may be essayed. With Strawson one may seek to disarm the divers locutions that tempt us to regard truth as a relation between independently specifiable entities.[1] With Rorty one may exhibit alleged intuitions about the nature of reference as philosophical misdescriptions of the largely conventional practices we adopt in interpreting the utterances of others.[2] With Dummett one may argue that the relation between truth and meaning is such as to rule out ascription of verification transcendent truth conditions on pain of rendering linguistic competence inexplicable.[3] With Putnam one may seek to refute the correspondence theory outright by proving the impossibility of unambiguous reference.[4]

More effective, perhaps, than analytical argument is the 'hermeneutics of suspicion'. With Nietzsche one may seek to unmask our commitment to 'the real world' as the ultimate standard of truth, tracing its theological pedigree and exposing its ignoble psychological roots.[5] With Dewey one may castigate the dualism of world and knowledge as 'conservative intellectualism', a product of philosophers' detachment from the domains of work and action.[6] With Heidegger one may show how the pristine apprehension of nature as elemental power that prevailed in the pre-Socratic dawn of philosophy, the lost fatherland of thought, degenerated into conceptions of nature as a prototype to be copied, imitated, or

---

[1] P. F. Strawson, 'Truth', *Proceedings of the Aristotelian Society*, suppl. vol. 24 (1950), 129–56; 'Truth: a reconsideration of Austin's views', *Philosophical Quarterly*, 15 (1965), 289–301.

[2] R. Rorty, 'Realism and reference', *The Monist*, 5 (1976), 321–40; *Philosophy and the Mirror of Nature*, Princeton, 1980, ch. 6.

[3] M. Dummett, 'What is a theory of meaning?', in S. Guttenplan, ed., *Mind and Language*, Oxford, 1975, 97–138; 'What is a theory of meaning? (II)', in G. Evans and J. McDowell, eds., *Truth and Meaning: Essays in Semantics*, Oxford, 1976, 67–137. For a damaging critique of Dummett's arguments see M. Devitt, *Realism and Truth*, Oxford, 1984, ch. 12.

[4] H. Putnam, 'Models and reality', *The Journal of Symbolic Logic*, 45 (1980), 464–82. Putnam's argument has been effectively countered by I. Hacking, *Representing and Intervening*, Cambridge, 1983, 101–8; Devitt, *Realism and Truth*, ch. 11; A. L. Brueckner, 'Putnam's model-theoretic argument against metaphysical realism', *Analysis*, 44 (1984), 134–40.

[5] On Nietzsche's onslaught on 'the world of true being' see R. Schacht, *Nietzsche*, London, 1983, 159–64.

[6] See, for example, J. Dewey, 'A short catechism concerning truth', in *The Influence of Darwin on Philosophy and other Essays in Contemporary Thought*, New York, 1910; *The Quest for Certainty. A Study of the Relation of Knowledge and Action*, New York, 1928, chs 1 and 2.

re-presented.[7] With Foucault one may expose distinctions between an 'order of words' and an 'order of things' as products of logophobia, fear of the subversive and anarchic potential of untrammelled discourse.[8]

To these variously efficacious ploys I venture to add one that may prove therapeutic for those who, whilst perhaps having reservations about correspondence theories of truth in other fields, find unproblematic the identification of truth in science as representation of the world 'as it is', undistorted by the standpoint of any observer. The concept of a scientific theory as a deductively integrated body of propositions related to a systematic practice of prediction, observation, and experiment appears in European thought, as I have argued elsewhere, only at the end of the sixteenth century. Its primary context of emergence is provided by astronomy and in particular by the then unresolved conflict between Ptolemaic, Copernican, and Tychonic cosmologies.[9] In this context the metaphor of truth as portrayal, modelling, or mirroring of the world is a live one. Each of the three chief world-systems can, when its planetary models have been fully specified, be regarded as a recipe for construction of a scale model of the universe—either a static one, a planetarium, or a kinematic one, an orrery. By metonymy world-systems themselves may be considered as models of the universe. In astronomy the distinction between true and apparent celestial locations and motions is explained by appeal to the earthbound standpoint of the observer and the laws of classical optics: this is so whether the preferred world-system be Ptolemaic, Tychonic, or Copernican, though of course the Copernican system greatly extends the gulf between appearance and reality thus to be explained. It is natural here to think of the true world-system as one which represents the world as it is, not as it variously appears from the standpoints of particular observers. In the kinematic astronomy of 1600, then, the metaphorical equation of truth with modelling, portrayal, or representation of the world as it is, not as it appears from any particular standpoint, is apt and compelling.

Typical scientific theories lack both the features that render the

[7] M. Heidegger, *An Introduction to Metaphysics*, trans R. Manheim, New Haven, 1959, 52–74.
[8] M. Foucault, *L'ordre du discours*, Paris, 1971; English trans. by I. McLeod in R. Young, ed., *Untying the Text: A Post-Structuralist Reader*, London, 1981, 51–76.
[9] N. Jardine, *The Birth of History and Philosophy of Science*, Cambridge, 1984, ch. 9.

image of truth as portrayal of the real world so effective in the case of celestial kinematics. Whilst recipes may be derived from many theories for construction of models of some part or aspect of the world, typical theories cannot be translated in their entireties into such recipes; and whilst it is often possible to maintain a relatively clear-cut distinction between the data on which a theory is based and the claims of the theory itself, it is rarely apposite to consider the data as the product of distortion by the observer's standpoint of the 'reality' postulated by the theory. The metaphor of truth as portrayal of the world as it really is seems on examination to be not only dead but also, for the majority of types of scientific theory, inept.

Now let us turn to an account of truth that prefigures our own in certain respects. On this account the standard of truth is the limit of human inquiry, the theory that would be converged on were human inquiry prosecuted indefinitely under sufficiently favourable circumstances.[10] I shall call this 'the limit-of-inquiry account'.

Consider an infinite series of theories generated by an indefinitely protracted inquiry. To find a sense in which such a series may have a limit we must find an appropriate analogue for numerical convergence. The simplest type of numerical convergence, Weierstrass

[10] The limit-of-inquiry account is commonly attributed to C. S. Peirce; but there is room for doubt whether the attribution is warranted. Peirce certainly held that science is convergent in the sense that 'the truth will out'—that is, true scientific hypotheses are such that sufficiently prolonged scientific inquiries would yield stable consensus on them. This claim is linked to the claim that scientific inquiry is self-corrective, in the sense that prolonged address to theoretical questions by scientific methods yields sequences of hypotheses that ever more closely approximate the true answers. But it is far from clear that Peirce held scientific consensuses as a whole to be convergent on an ultimate theory. Interesting treatments of these aspects of Peirce's thought are to be found in L. Laudan, 'Peirce and the trivialization of the self-corrective thesis', in R. N. Giere and R. S. Westfall, eds., *Foundations of Scientific Method: The Nineteenth Century*, Bloomington, Indiana, 1973, 275–306; C. Hookway, *Peirce*, London, 1985, chs. 2, 7, and 8; and R. Almeder, 'Peirce's thirteen theories of truth', *Transactions of the Charles S. Peirce Society*, 21 (1985), 77–94. In the writings of Wilfrid Sellars and Jay F. Rosenberg the conceptual scheme on which an ideal human inquiry would converge figures as a repository of truth. In Sellars, however, the ultimate standard of truth remains correctness of portrayal of the world, whereas in Rosenberg the real world is explicated as that which is portrayed by the limiting theory: W. Sellars, *Science, Perception and Reality*, London, 1963; J. F. Rosenberg, *Linguistic Representation*, Dordrecht, 1974, and 'Transcendental arguments and pragmatic epistemology', in P. Bieri *et al.*, eds., *Transcendental Arguments and Science*, Dordrecht, 1979, 245–62. The Sellarsian approach is modified and developed by I. Niiniluoto, 'Scientific progress', in *Is Science Progressive?*, Dordrecht, 1984, 75–110.

convergence, is that according to which a sequence of numbers $r_1 \ldots r_n \ldots$ converges on limit L just in case for any number ε, however small, we can by going far enough along the series reach a point beyond which every member of the series is at or within ε of L. That is:

$$(\varepsilon) \ (\exists n^*)(n)(n > n^* \to |r_n - L| \leqslant \varepsilon).$$

On this model, convergence of a series of theories on theory T occurs just in case for any degree of approximation ε, however close, one can by going far enough along the series reach a point beyond which every theory approximates T to degree ε or more closely. This sort of convergence cannot be used to specify a limiting theory since it presupposes its specification. Cauchy convergence is more promising. Here a sequence of numbers converges just in case for any number ε, however small, one can by going far enough along the series reach a point beyond which all pairs of numbers differ by ε or less. That is:

$$(\varepsilon)(\exists n^*)(n)(n')(n > n^* \ \& \ n' > n^* \to |r_n - r_{n'}| \leqslant \varepsilon).$$

On this model, convergence of a series of theories on theory T occurs just in case for any degree of approximation ε, however close, one can by going far enough along the series reach a point beyond which any two theories approximate each other to degree ε or more closely.[11]

Serious difficulties beset the attempt to use an analogue of Cauchy convergence to explicate the notion of a limit of human inquiry. As it stands the proposed analogue of Cauchy convergence requires a numerical measure of similarity ranging over theories. It seems most unlikely that such a measure is to be had.[12] Comparisons of similarities between pairs of theories in different domains of inquiry generally appear nonsensical. It is surely senseless, for example, to claim that Mendel's factor theory is more similar to Morgan's mathematical genetics than classical celestial mechanics is to special relativistic celestial mechanics. Further, even if we confine ourselves to local comparisons—that is, comparisons of the similarities of a given theory to other theories—numerical judgements appear senseless. It would surely be absurd,

[11] Cf. J. F. Rosenberg, *Linguistic Representation*, Dordrecht, 1974, p. 94.

[12] Cf. W. V. O. Quine, 'The pragmatists' place in empiricism', in R. J. Mulvaney and P. M. Zeltner, eds., *Pragmatism: Its Sources and Prospects*, Columbia, South Carolina, 1981, 21–39, p. 31.

for example, to claim that Morgan's mathematical genetics is twice as similar to Mendel's factor theory as it is to Benzer's fine-structure genetics. It does appear, however, that we are on occasion entitled to local ordinal judgements of similarity between theories, that is, judgements of the form 'T_1 is more similar to T_2 than it is to T_3'. This is not, by itself, enough to enable us to contrive an analogue of Cauchy convergence; but it is on the cards that with sufficient ingenuity measures of intertheoretic similarity with a bit more structure could be so contrived as to allow construction of an analogue. The notion of an ultimate theory lying at the limit of human inquiry is, I submit, if not fully intelligible, at least closely enough verging on intelligibility for examination of its other credentials to be well worth while.

Let us consider first the empirical adequacy of the claim that there is a limit of human inquiry, then the capacity of such a limit to serve as the standard of truth. The history of science tends to disconfirm the hypothesis that the human inquiry series is convergent on a limiting theory. We can, indeed, detect many cases of ever closer approximation to present theories by temporally successive past theories. But this does not suffice as evidence for convergence on a limit. To obtain that we would have to detect diminishing returns with the passage of time, a general deceleration of progress as estimated from the standpoint of current theories. No such tendency is discernible.[13] Indeed, despite great unevenness in rates of change and great disparities between different fields, a case could surely be made for the converse tendency, a general acceleration of change as estimated from the standpoint of current theories.

If the history of science fails to yield evidence for convergence of human inquiry on a limiting theory, why have claims about the convergence of human inquiry achieved so wide a currency? A number of explanations, some charitable, some less so, spring to mind. For example, one may be led astray by a hasty extrapolation from the many cases in which successive past estimates of some parameter (for example, the refractive index of water or the distance of the sun) show convergence on the currently accepted estimate. Another tempting basis for extrapolation is provided by cases in which inquiry within the bounds of some particular theory, paradigm, or research programme has yielded diminishing returns as the problems that can be posed within that framework are

---

[13] Cf. N. Rescher, *The Limits of Science*, Berkeley, 1984, ch. 2.

exhausted. These two sorts of evidence for diminishing returns combine to potentially misleading effect in cases where ever more precise and complete models of the 'machinery' underlying the phenomena are achieved through application of an underlying theory to increasingly refined observation and/or experiment—think, for example, of the ever more precise working out of the planetary orbits within the framework of Newtonian celestial mechanics or of the ever more accurate mapping of the fruit-fly genome within the framework of classical genetics. It is this that may lend a specious plausibility to the claim that 'theoretical progress is marked by the *decreasing* slack with which successive theories fit *increasingly refined* data'.[14] To undermine this claim it suffices to turn our attention from Kuhnian normal science to interludes of revolutionary science—the shift from classical to relativistic celestial mechanics or the shift from classical to fine-structure genetics, for example. Here there is little to encourage the view that progress is marked by decreasing slack between theories and the phenomena. (In this connection it is noteworthy that the heydays of strong claims about the convergence of science on an ultimate theory, the opening and closing decades of the nineteenth century, mark the ends of periods of relative Kuhnian 'normality' in the exact sciences.[15]) Yet another source of confidence in convergence of inquiry on a limit may be its confusion with a type of convergence that is prevalent in the history of science, namely, convergence of belief. This type of convergence, the emergence of consensus from agnosticism or disparity in belief, I shall, to avoid confusion, call 'concurrence'. Concurrence will play a considerable role in the following chapters; but for the moment it suffices to note that whilst the prevalence of concurrence is indeed a necessary condition for convergence of the human inquiry series on a limit, it is far from sufficient.

Let us now consider whether, even supposing the human inquiry series to be genuinely convergent on a limit, the limiting theory thus defined would suffice as a standard of truth. On two counts it appears that it would not.

---

[14] Rosenberg, *Linguistic Representation*, p. 94, author's emphases.

[15] On the Laplacian vision of an all-encompassing mechanics see, e.g., R. Fox, 'The rise and fall of Laplacian physics', *Historical Studies in the Physical Sciences*, 4 (1974), 89–136. On late nineteenth-century premonitions of the imminent unification and completion of theoretical science see L. Badash, 'The completeness of nineteenth-century science', *Isis*, 63 (1972), 48–58.

If the human inquiry series really does manifest convergence, may not the successively smaller steps that are achieved in successive intervals of time represent an inevitable bogging-down of inquiry rather than an asymptotic approach to the whole truth? Indeed, it may be asked, what better indication could there be of the existence of limitations on our cognitive capacities than the discovery that we are fated to achieve ever diminishing returns for our inquisitive efforts? It seems that the definition of a limit of human inquiry that we have sketched is at least consistent with, if not suggestive of, an interpretation of that limit as constituted not by a body of truth, but by a theory affected by errors and limitations that we humans cannot, given the imperfections of our sensory and intellectual capacities, surpass. Further, such a definition of a limit of inquiry seems not to pre-empt claims to the effect that that limit represents not truth, but rather a consensus conditioned by the particular vantage points of the creators and curators of scientific theories. Would not the human inquiry series tend to a rather different limit had Marcellus' soldiers spared Archimedes in his sand-pit? Would not the series tend to a very different limit had systematic theorizing about the world originated in China rather than Ionia? Would not the series tend to an immeasurably different limit were humans to have been in consultation with the hyper-intelligent, X-ray eyed, gravitation-flux sensitive, denizens of Canopus?

The protagonist of the limit of inquiry account of truth may try to counter these challenges by offering further specifications of the hypothetical limiting theory. In the attempt to avoid the first objection one cannot, on pain of circularity in the account of truth, insist outright that the limiting theory be immune to all types of error. One may, however, impose a strong coherence condition, insisting that the limiting theory include an explicit account of the sources of human error and a demonstration of the immunity against those sources of error of the methods by which it itself is derived. Alas, strong though this requirement looks, it is surely insufficient. Like Mr Elton in Jane Austen's *Emma*, whose inferiority in talent supposedly prevented him from recognizing his inferiority in talent, so those who hold theories that are infected with error may well be blinded thereby to their predicament. Thus a limiting theory might well satisfy the condition trivially because, whilst it was able to show its own immunity to all the sources of error recognizable from its standpoint, its standpoint was one from which few sources of error were discernible. Further, where the history of science is distinctly inhospitable to the view that there exists a limit of human inquiry, it positively militates against the existence of a limit of this self-vindicating sort. From the standpoint of our theories we can, to be sure, see how sources of systematic error and limitation, at first unrecognized, have been detected and then eliminated or controlled. But far from providing inductive grounds for supposing that the process of transcendence of sources of error and limitation would, were inquiry to continue indefinitely, tend to demonstrable completion, it suggests that there is no end to this process of detection and subsequent avoidance or evasion of sources of error.

To escape the second objection it would be necessary to show that the theory which lies at the actual limit of human inquiry lies also at the limit of all possible suitably conducted inquiries, whether they be the inquiries of non-human intelligences, or the inquiries that humans might have conducted under hypothetically varied courses of history. Quite apart from the difficulties that would arise in specifying what in this context constitutes a 'suitably conducted inquiry', this seems a hopeless task. Just as the history of science provides our sole source of evidence on which to assess the claim that the human inquiry series has a limit, so it is our only source of evidence germane to the far bolder claim that all 'suitably conducted' inquiries have the same limit. The historical evidence that militates against the former hypothesis militates likewise against the latter.

The failure of this attempt to use the limit of human inquiry as a standard of truth is instructive. On the one hand the account fails because it pays insufficient attention to the nature of the history of science. The convergence hypothesis is an unwarranted extrapolation from just one aspect of that history, the successive approximations of earlier theories to later ones. But if the proposed standard of truth is in this respect too remote from the actual fortunes of human inquiry, it remains in another and crucial respect too close to them. In tying truth to a particular, albeit hypothetical, outcome of human inquiry it fails to define a truth that is unconditioned by error, distortion, or partiality.

The pragmatic account of truth to be offered in the next chapter is modelled on the limit-of-inquiry account in crucial respects: it too attempts to explicate truth in terms of the fortunes of inquiry; and it too is answerable to evidence drawn from the history of science. My hope is that, by taking into account more aspects of the history of science and by extrapolating from those aspects more cautiously, an explication can be achieved that does justice at once to truth's immanence in history and to truth's transcendence of error and distortion.

III

Truth and Inquiry

THE pragmatic 'limit-of-inquiry' account of truth depends, as we have seen, on the untenable view that the history of science manifests a tendency towards an ultimate complete theory. Yet, so I have argued, the account still fails to guarantee the transcendence of error and independence of standpoint that are constitutive of the notion of truth. If even so strong and unrealistic an interpretation of the history of science is unable to ground a notion of truth as unconditioned by error or standpoint, how can we hope to succeed in this task on the basis of a moderate and realistic interpretation?

The hunch on which the following account is based is that to obtain secular materials for the explication of truth and the defence of scientific absolutism we must appeal to many different aspects of the history of science. We shall make no single demand on the history of science comparable in stringency with the demand for sequential convergence of consensually accepted theories on an ultimate theory, but we shall make many less stringent demands.

Much of our concern with the history of science will be focused on the ways in which temporal sequences of theories may be interpreted from the standpoints of later theories, and especially from the standpoint of our own theories. Thus we shall be interested in cases in which questions posed at earlier stages of inquiry appear from the standpoints of later theories to have been either determined, that is, answered one way or the other, or dissolved, that is, shown to be ill-posed because they rest on false presuppositions or because they are not susceptible to evidential considerations.[1] Consider a couple of questions raised by medieval cosmologists. Is Mercury nearer to Earth than is Venus? Does the external

---

[1] The requisite notion of presupposition is far from transparent. What matters for our purposes is the generally agreed point that if $Q?$ presupposes p and p is false, then there is no true direct answer to $Q?$ (cf. N. B. Belnap and T. B. Steel, *The Logic of Questions and Answers*, New Haven, 1976, ch. 3). Further explication of the notion runs into a series of well-known difficulties concerning the status of assertions whose presuppositions are false—on some accounts false, on others truth-valueless or

mover of a heavenly orb act uniformly on the entire orb or rather concentrate its activity around the planet which the orb carries? From the standpoint of modern astronomy we see the first of these questions as having been determined with the establishment of Copernican cosmology and the second as having been dissolved, Tycho Brahe's refutation of the existence of substantial celestial orbs having shown it to rest on a false presupposition. Again, consider questions about the types of cosmic weather that correspond to particular bodily diseases. In the context of a Paracelsian world-view such questions are in principle determinable by appeal to the bodily signs of diseases. Such determination depends upon diagnosis through divine illumination of the emblematic significances of the bodily signs. From the standpoints of later scientific consensuses such questions are ill posed because the methods by which it was supposed that evidence might be brought to bear on them are seen as unsound. (It should be noted that these modes of dissolution will often affect substantial bodies of questions *en bloc*. Thus when from the standpoint of later theories theoretical entities postulated by their predecessors are non-existent, extensive ranges of questions that presuppose the existence of those entities may be dissolved. Similarly, when from the standpoint of later theories methods for the determination of questions associated with earlier theories are seen as unsound, substantial bodies of questions whose determinability depended on those methods may be dissolved.) We shall be interested too in cases in which from the standpoint of later theories it appears that sources of error in the construction of earlier hypotheses or theories were in due course recognized and overcome. Thus, from the standpoint of current astronomy it appears that Copernicus' complex account of precession was based on a distorted chronology of ancient observations and that Tycho Brahe, who recognized this source of error, provided an account which avoids it. Above all we shall be interested in cases of successive approximation in content to later theories in temporal sequences of theories.

possessed of a truth value other than true or false. Difficulties are posed too by questions and assertions with more than one level of presupposition. Yet more difficulties arise on the score of demarcation of strict or 'semantic' presupposition from the various types of preparatory conditions for speech acts and context dependent implications that are often lumped together as 'pragmatic' presuppositions. The wide range of views on these issues is well represented in Ch.-K. Oh and D. A. Dinneen, eds., *Presupposition*, New York, 1979.

Other historical processes to which we shall appeal are ones that have ensued from contact between distinct lines or traditions of inquiry. Thus we shall be much concerned with cases of 'domination' in which one tradition of inquiry yields what its exponents purport to be valid explanations of divergences between its deliverances and those of some other tradition of inquiry, the explanations being in terms of systematic errors or limitations afflicting that other line of inquiry. Sometimes this will be a local affair concerning particular lines of inquiry within a single tradition. Here, for example, belongs the explanation by Mendelian geneticists of the divergences between De Vries's saltationist genetics and 'orthodox' genetics in terms of De Vries and his co-workers having been misled by the anomalous breeding system of the Evening Primrose. At the other extreme is the case where one entire tradition of inquiry has dominated another. Here would belong, for example, an explanation of divergences between the fruits of Arabic and European cosmological inquiry, on the one hand, and the fruits of classical Chinese cosmological inquiry, on the other, that appealed to the limited empirical basis of the Chinese speculations. We shall be concerned too with the assimilation that occurs when one line of inquiry overcomes the divergences between its outcomes and those of another by appropriating the divergent beliefs. Here, for example, belongs the assimilation of Newtonian physics into the curricula of French educational institutions previously committed to Cartesian physics that took place in the middle of the eighteenth century; and here, to take a more dramatic example, belongs the rapid assimilation of European astronomy into a radically divergent tradition of astronomical inquiry after its introduction to China by Jesuit missionaries at the beginning of the seventeenth century.

Concurrence of belief is perhaps the most diverse of all the categories of historical development to which we shall appeal. It occurs whenever consensus in belief emerges from agnosticism or disparity in belief. The type of concurrence that will be of primary interest to us is that in which beliefs we hold have had multiple independent origins, either because they originated also in traditions of investigation other than that which gave rise to our science, or because they originated from independent inquiries or types of research within that tradition. This sort of concurrence covers cases of independent formulation of hypotheses, theories, or explanations. Here, for example, belong the independent discoveries of the Metonic and Callippic cycles (periodicities in the apparent locations of heavenly bodies) by the Babylonians and Chinese, the independent statements of Snel's law of refraction by Snel and Descartes, and the independent explanations of the acoustic Doppler effect by Christiaan Doppler and Hippolyte Fizeau. It covers also cases in which identical or near-identical estimates of values of parameters have been derived from different data and different experimental techniques. A typical example is the congruence of estimates of Avogadro's number based on observations of Brownian motion with those derived from study of black-body radiation.

Appeal to these categories of historical development involves retrospective judgements, both in the picking out of traditions of inquiry ancestral to modern science and in the assessment of past theories from the standpoint of current theories. Is not such a 'presentist' and 'judgemental' approach to past systems of belief at odds with the new historiography of science celebrated in the introduction to this work? First, it must be conceded outright that a historian who concentrated exclusively, or even predominantly, on the processes listed above would be apt to produce dismal chronicles. But it should go without saying that a philosopher's interests may diverge widely from those of historians. If the processes on which we shall focus serve well our interests in the defence of scientific absolutism, we need not be disturbed by their inadequacies as motifs in serious historiography. It would, however, be fatal to our enterprise were it demonstrable that the processes to whose prevalence we shall appeal are rare or absent from the history of science. In this connection it may be noted pre-emptively that our claims about successive approximation of earlier theories to later (and, in particular, present) theories are fully consistent with such accumulation of content having been uneven, piecemeal, and subject to temporary reversals.[2] Were this not so our use of the history of science would run foul of historical common sense, or rather of common sense informed by post-Kuhnian historiography of science. Further salient threats are posed by two theses closely

---

[2] Cf. the contrast drawn between short- and long-run accumulation by G. Doppelt, 'Kuhn's epistemological relativism: an interpretation and defence', in J. W. Meiland and M. Krausz, eds., *Relativism, Cognitive and Moral*, Notre Dame, Indiana, 1982, 113–48.

associated with the new historiography, the thesis of incommensurability of theories and the thesis of indeterminacy of intertheoretic interpretation, which if conceded outright surely invalidate all claims to discern the historical processes sketched above. The attempt to meet these threats is deferred until we have set out our pragmatic account of truth and our preliminary historical defence of scientific absolutism.

We now set about the explication of truth.

Let us say that S is true given theory T just in case S is in T. Infinite temporally indexed sequences of theories will be called '(infinite) inquiry series', 'infinite' being specified only in contexts where failure to do so might engender confusion with finite inquiry series. 'Theory' is intended here in a very broad sense, including not only theories in the sense customary in scientific usage, but also large conjunctions of theories, principles and hypotheses, entire world-pictures. The properties of inquiry series that will mainly concern us are ones whose possession is possible only for series of theories of such wide scope, ranging over many scientific disciplines and including both first-order beliefs and beliefs about sources of error, means for the reliable resolution of questions, and proper modes of explanation.

For the sake of brevity we shall write 'X is Y given T' for ' "X is Y" is true given T'. For example, 'E is a source of error given T' abbreviates ' "E is a source of error" is true given T'. The main scheme to be used in building up our account is as follows. S is true from the standpoint of inquiry series $\emptyset$ just in case there exists i such that, for all $T_{i',i}$ in $\emptyset$, S is true given $T_{i'}$. Informally stated, something is true from the standpoint of an inquiry series just in case there is a stage in the series beyond which every theory in the series contains it.

A simple question $Q?$ is determined by $\emptyset$ just in case either Q is true from the standpoint of $\emptyset$ or $\sim Q$ is true from the standpoint of $\emptyset$. As indicated earlier, we take well-posedness of questions to depend both on the truth of their presuppositions and on their susceptibility to evidential considerations. So we say that a question $Q?$ is well posed from the standpoint of T just in case given T its presuppositions are true and it is susceptible to evidential considerations. (The dependence on background theory of susceptibility to evidential considerations is a complex matter. Thus background theory is involved in determining what may be counted as evidence; it is involved in determining what methods and criteria may be used to tackle questions in the light of evidence; and it is involved because it may contribute premises that combine with evidence to cast light on questions. It should be emphasized that on the present account the well-posedness of a question given a theory does not require its susceptibility given that theory to conclusive or near conclusive evidential considerations; nor does it require that given that theory relevant evidence be accessible to inquiries, nor that the evidential considerations to which the question is susceptible given that theory be empirical considerations.) An inquiry series $\emptyset$ is *infinitely resolutive of questions* just in case, for all $Q?$ such that $Q?$ is well posed from the standpoint of $\emptyset$, $Q?$ is determined by $\emptyset$. Informally stated, an inquiry series infinitely resolutive of questions is one from the standpoint of which no genuine question for ever resists settlement.

Infinite resolution of questions is a notion derived by extrapolation from the finite historical processes of determination and dissolution of questions that may be discerned from the standpoint of our theories. By an analogous extrapolation we may derive the notion of infinite transcendence of error; though the extrapolation is slightly more complex, since theoretical standpoint conditions not only judgements about what constitute sources of error, but also judgements about which theories overcome which sources of error. Accordingly, we say that a source of error E is overcome by $\emptyset$ just in case there exists i such that, for all $T_{i',i}$ in $\emptyset$, $T_{i'}$ overcomes E from the standpoint of $\emptyset$. $\emptyset$ is *infinitely transcendent of error* just in case, for all E such that E is a source of error from the standpoint of $\emptyset$, E is overcome by $\emptyset$. Informally stated, a series infinitely transcendent of error is one from the standpoint of which there are no ineluctable sources of error.

An inquiry series that is both infinitely resolutive of questions and infinitely transcendent of error is one that is from its own internal standpoint subject to no cognitive limitations. Let us call such an inquiry series 'internally unbounded'. There is an obvious hiatus between truth from the standpoint of an internally unbounded inquiry series and truth, with its immunity to every conceivable source of error, bias, and limitation. Internally unbounded inquiry series may include, for example, series relative to which only the most undemanding of questions are well posed or from whose standpoints few, if any, sources of error are recognized. Less trivially, they may include inquiry series that are, by our lights, systematically infected with errors of types that remain for ever concealed from the inquirers themselves by protective 'secondary elaborations'. Consider, for example, inquirers whose inquiries consist in exegesis and commentary of the texts of some sage of their antiquity. When faced with apparent discrepancies between the fruits of their own investigations and the doctrines of their authority, these inquirers react like oysters troubled by sand: they contrive ever more complex theories about the corruptions and interpolations to which those texts may have been exposed. Thus they are everlastingly insulated from recognition of their own subservience to authority as a source of systematic error. To take an example of another familiar category, imagine inquirers unshakeably committed to a metaphysical system that distinguishes sharply between a transcendent and immutable real world and a phenomenal world that is chaotic and indeterminate. From our standpoint their inquiries are seen never to resolve a host of well-posed questions about the phenomenal world. But from the standpoint of their inquiries these questions are resolved *en bloc*: all are declared ill posed on the grounds that they falsely presuppose the regularity and determinacy of the phenomena.

There is, of course, room for doubt about the possibility of certain of these 'misguided' but internally unbounded inquiry series. On the one hand, in the cases that predicate drastic cognitive limitations of the hypothetical inquirers, it may be wondered whether such cognitively impoverished beings can coherently be supposed to be users of language, let alone inquirers. On the other hand, once the hypothetical inquirers are credited with even a modicum of procedure that is by our standards reliable, it may become hard to sustain the supposition that they could persist indefinitely in their use of other procedures that are by our lights unreliable. It seems most unlikely, however, that these reservations can be built up into a general argument for the impossibility of internally unbounded but by our lights misguided inquiry series.

The forms of inquiry that reveal the hiatus between truth and truth from the standpoint of an internally unbounded inquiry series are by hypothesis unsatisfactory from the standpoint of our current beliefs. In each case we can give a partial account or explanation of the origin and maintenance of the alien inquirers' beliefs. And in each case the account we give is such as to show their inquiries to be, by our lights, limited in their capacity to resolve questions and/or subject to systematic error. Extrapolating from such cases, we offer a tentative account of the way in which one entire inquiry series may have, from the standpoint of another, a limited capacity to resolve questions and/or transcend error. We say that inquiry series $\emptyset$, $\emptyset'$ are *ultimately divergent* just in case, for some $Q?$, the status of $Q?$ given $\emptyset$—ill posed, well posed and determined in the affirmative, well posed and determined in the negative, well posed and open, issue of well-posedness open—differs from its status given $\emptyset'$. $\emptyset$ *dominates* $\emptyset'$ in case $\emptyset$ and $\emptyset'$ are ultimately divergent and there exists an explanation or set of explanations E, true from the standpoint of $\emptyset$, which explains the whole of the divergence in terms of error and/or limitation in the procedures of inquiry that generate $\emptyset'$. $\emptyset$ is *absolutely dominant* in the case in which it dominates all ultimately divergent inquiry series but is itself dominated by none. Informally stated, an absolutely dominant inquiry series is one from the standpoint of which all ultimately divergent inquiry series can be 'explained away', but which cannot itself be 'explained away' from the standpoint of any ultimately divergent inquiry series.

We are now in a position to specify a type of inquiry series worthy to serve as a standard for truth. An absolute inquiry series is characterized by the following: infinite transcendence of error; infinite resolution of questions; absolute dominance. Note that ultimate divergence between absolute inquiry series is impossible. To see this suppose a pair of absolute inquiry series to be ultimately divergent. Since each is absolute, each must be absolutely dominant. So, impossibly, each must dominate the other and each must be undominated by the other.

We explicate truth as follows. S is *true* if, and only if, there is an absolute inquiry series from the standpoint of which it is true.

Note that since ultimate divergence between absolute inquiry series is impossible, what is true from the standpoint of an absolute inquiry series is true from the standpoints of all absolute inquiry series.

As a first step in the defence of our account let us consider two pressing objections on the score of intelligibility.

The crucial notion of an absolute inquiry series is derived by extrapolation from, and purports to have its intelligibility grounded in, processes that have occurred in the history of human inquiry.

Thus infinite transcendence of error and infinite resolution of questions are extrapolations of the finite historical processes of error transcendence and resolution of questions detectable from the standpoint of current theories. Absolute dominance is similarly derived by extrapolation, this time from asymmetrical explanatory relationships between lines of inquiry ancestral to our science and certain other lines of inquiry. It is on the score of infinite resolution of questions that the most obvious challenge to intelligibility arises. How many coelacanths swam in the deeps, how many pterodactyls flitted the skies and how many tyrannosaurs roamed the earth eighty million years ago today? That many such questions have determinate answers is an assumption that we are exceedingly unlikely to revise. But it is practically certain that almost all such questions would remain unresolved even were human inquiry (or, for that matter, the inquiries of whatever other inquirers the universe may sustain) to continue for ever. For we have no reason to suppose that there is now extant information from which the number of pterodactyls around just eighty million years ago is recoverable. And we have good reason to believe time-travel to be physically, if not conceptually, impossible.[3] Mere persistence of address to the question, even by beings with sensory and cognitive capacities immensely outdistancing our own, could not guarantee that an answer would be forthcoming.[4]

Suppose we start out by thinking of inquiry series as simple temporal extrapolations of the outcomes of actual finite inquiries. On this initial conception it is very hard to see how an inquiry series could be infinitely resolutive of questions. For there are genuine questions that could almost certainly be determined only by investigators who had access to evidence that is inaccessible to any physically possible investigator under any physically possible circumstances. For example, it is, as noted above, very unlikely that any physically possible inquirer could under any physically possible conditions of inquiry

[3] An ingenious argument for the conceptual impossibility of time-travel is to be found in D. H. Mellor, *Real Time*, Cambridge, 1981.

[4] The analogous case of facts once observed but destined to be forgotten was raised by Russell and Ayer against the limit-of-inquiry account of truth that they attributed to Peirce: see B. Russell, 'Dewey's new logic', in P. A. Schilpp, ed., *The Philosophy of John Dewey*, Evanston and Chicago, 1939, 139–56, and A. J. Ayer, *The Origins of Pragmatism*, Glasgow, 1963, ch. 2. H. Field, 'Realism and relativism', *The Journal of Philosophy*, 79 (1982), 553–67, wields the objection against the view of truth as idealized rational acceptability defended by H. Putnam in *Reason, Truth and History*, Cambridge, 1981.

obtain evidence sufficient for the resolution of questions about the precise sizes of past pterodactyl populations. To put infinite resolution of questions by an inquiry series on the cards we must, it seems, conceive of inquiry series with a good deal more counterfactual bravado. In particular we must imaginatively escape from the spatio-temporal limitations on the evidence-gathering capacities of ourselves and other physically possible inquirers. The fiction of time-travel provides, I suggest, precisely what is needed. Let us call an investigation by beings with spatio-temporally unlimited evidence-gathering capacities 'evidentially unrestricted'. Inquiry series may then be thought of as the products of infinitely protracted and evidentially unrestricted investigations, those investigations being as like to those carried out by physically possible inquirers under physically possible circumstances as is consistent with their endless protraction and freedom from evidential restrictions.

A second pressing objection on the score of intelligibility concerns absolute dominance. The difficulty here arises from inquiry series that, whilst from the standpoint of our beliefs about proper procedures of inquiry obviously misguided, appear to have the capacity to dominate all divergent inquiry series. An inquiry series of this sort, at once obviously dominated and dominating all divergent inquiry series, would rule out the possibility of an inquiry series that, itself undominated, dominated all other inquiry series; hence it would rule out the possibility of an absolute inquiry series. Such apparent 'dogs-in-the-manger' are obtained by endowing with modest degrees of self-reflection the obviously misguided but internally unbounded inquiry series mentioned earlier. Consider again the case of an inquiry series generated by exegesis and commentary of the texts of some sage of an alien antiquity. Now suppose that in addition to the first-order fruits of commentary and exegesis certain second-order claims be true from the standpoint of the inquiry series—for instance, the claim that beliefs generated by scholarly and critical exegesis and commentary of the canonical texts are generally reliable and that procedures of inquiry that give rise to conclusions at odds with, or unrepresented amongst, the doctrines of the canonical texts are generally unreliable. Thus enriched with reflective claims the inquiry series appears to have the capacity to dominate all divergent inquiry series, by providing explanations for the divergences in terms of systematic error in the procedures that give rise to them.

Care is needed in attempting to meet this objection. On pain of circularity we cannot simply rule out as not properly explanatory the explanations of divergence provided by such inquiry series. Nor, it seems, can we find grounds independent of our convictions about what constitute reliable methods of inquiry for constraining the kinds of explanations that may make an inquiry series dominant. A better line of resistance challenges not the status or content of the explanations provided by such apparently all-dominating inquiry series, but rather the possibility of such inquiry series. Earlier, certain doubts were raised about the possibility of internally unbounded inquiry series generated by what are, by our lights, unreliable procedures. These doubts are reinforced in the present case by a consideration which arises when we consider the predicament of one who would explain discrepancies between his own system of beliefs and an alien system in such a way as to dominate the latter. On the one hand, the would-be explainer needs the ability to find out precisely what the alien beliefs are. On the other hand, he must bring to bear a theory of error. In the case of hypothetical 'misguided' but all-dominating inquiry series it seems that the first condition cannot be met; inquirers whose theory and practice of inquiry were thus permanently blinkered could not come to understand the majority of our theoretical beliefs, let alone the beliefs of whatever more advanced inquirers the universe may sustain.

There are a number of further scores on which qualms about the intelligibility of our account may persist. In particular, it may be objected that the notion of theoryhood on which the account is based stands itself in need of explication and that the notion of the well-posedness of a question from the standpoint of a theory has been inadequately specified. Thus in relating the well-posedness of questions to theories it was tacitly assumed that all the various conditions that together determine the range of questions that are well posed for a community of inquirers C, conditions of the form 'Evidence of type E would contribute to determination of Q?', can be considered as components of a theory held by members of C. In the following chapters it will be much emphasized that the criteria that are used to resolve theoretical questions are often tacitly adopted by inquirers, being revealed in their practices of inquiry rather than in their explicitly held methodologies. So the notion of theoryhood invoked in our account must be very broadly construed not only in the sense, already noted, that theories are to be allowed to include both first-order beliefs and beliefs about means for the resolution of questions, but also in the sense that they are to be allowed to include tacit beliefs and commitments. A fuller articulation and defence of our account would, therefore, have to take on hard questions about the nature of tacit belief and the grounds of its attribution.[5]

Let us turn now from the issue of intelligibility to another primary condition of adequacy for an account of truth, namely that it should exhibit truth as entirely uncontaminated with error and as entirely undistorted by the standpoint of any particular type of inquirers.

Freedom of truth from contamination by error and limitation is partly ensured, on our account, by the requirement that an absolute inquiry series be internally unbounded. This guarantees that it be such that from its own internal standpoint no ineluctable sources of error or limitation are discernible. As noted above, satisfaction of this internal condition is unimpressive should the inquiry series be one whose capacity to discern error and limitation is itself limited. But when in addition an inquiry series satisfies the absolute dominance condition, as must an absolute inquiry series, the internal condition becomes very much more powerful. For the absolute dominance condition can be satisfied only by an inquiry series that is asymmetrically related to all ultimately divergent inquiry series with respect to its powers of diagnosis of error, being such that: (i) no ultimately divergent inquiry series generates

---

[5] In connection with the notion of a theory the suspicion may arise that attempts at further explication would reveal circularity in our account of truth arising from the need to invoke the notions of consistency and derivability. Outright circularity in definition could, of course, be avoided by use of proof-theoretic treatments of consistency and derivability. But the objection does point up a major incompleteness in our account, namely, that no indication has been given of the way in which to elaborate semantic apparatus in which the validity and soundness of rules of inference may be investigated. The incompleteness is a serious one; for our account would clearly be called in question were it shown to block this kind of justification of standard deductive practices. (On the justificatory role of proofs of soundness and validity see M. Dummett, *The Justification of Deduction*, London, 1973.) Though I lack the competence to demonstrate the point by setting up the requisite semantic apparatus and proving the requisite metalogical theorems, my hunch is that the account is not vulnerable on this score. (I am encouraged in this hope by H. Putnam's account of the way in which classical propositional logic and its classical semantics may be preserved in the context of a 'quasi-intuitionistic' account of truth in terms of provability in a theory, through appropriate non-standard interpretation of the logical connectives: *Meaning and the Moral Sciences*, London, 1978, 24–9.)

explanations of the divergences in terms of its liability to error; (ii) it generates such explanations in respect of all inquiry series that are ultimately divergent from it.

As noted earlier, what is true from the standpoint of one absolute inquiry series cannot but be true from the standpoints of all absolute inquiry series. This is a crucial feature of our account; for it is in virtue of this eventual concurrence of all absolute inquiry series that our account satisfies the requirement that truth be exhibited as absolute in the sense of being undistorted by the standpoint of any particular inquirer or type of inquirers.

Given the many counts on which the history of science shows human inquiry to have been prone to error and distortion, it would be undesirable for an account of truth to tie it too closely to particular outcomes of human inquiry. Later I shall argue that the most extreme form of fallibilism, that which concedes to the sceptic the possibility that all our beliefs may be false, is not compatible with the account; but that there is nothing in the account to gainsay strong fallibilist claims to the effect that an enormous number of our most tenaciously held beliefs, perhaps all of them in certain scientific domains, may be false. Further, the account is consistent not only with the insecurity of our apprehension of truths, but also with strong claims about the epistemic elusiveness of truth. It does, indeed, preclude a certain extreme and hypothetical kind of elusiveness of truth, being incompatible with the existence of truths inaccessible to all possible inquirers, even given infinite time for the prosecution of their inquiries and their freedom from spatiotemporal restrictions on the gathering of evidence. But it is compatible with the existence of truths that are beyond the reach of all physically possible investigations, whether of humans or of inquirers of other types. It is not, I think, constitutive of the notion of truth that it should transcend the particular outcomes of inquiry in these ways; but an account of truth which precluded its epistemic insecurity and elusiveness would be under grave suspicion of having failed to underwrite the freedom from error and limitation that are genuinely constitutive of the notion of truth.

A further objection is likely to emanate from the more traditional sort of pragmatist. Whilst applauding the intimate linking of truth with the fortunes of inquiry, such an objector may well be perplexed by the failure to specify the kind of inquiry that is productive of truth. Should not the standard of truth be set by inquiries conducted in accordance with the canons of rational or scientific inquiry? Indeed it may even be argued that to tie the notion of truth to eventual consensus whilst failing to insist that the consensus be one reached by rational means is to yield to mob rule rather than reason as the arbiter of truth. Considerations to be adduced later in this work suggest that we are bound to decline this invitation. It will be argued that there are no universally applicable, theoretical context-free 'canons of rational inquiry'; at best we can hope to articulate locally applicable and theoretical context dependent criteria for the assessment of theories. Further, the reliability of such criteria can be warranted only a posteriori by appeal to their capacity to pick out theories whose truth is certified on independent grounds. No general recipe for rational inquiry can be given, beyond the purely schematic injunction to apply reliable methods, that is, methods apt to engender acceptance of truths; and that is a recipe that we cannot, on pain of circularity, appeal to in our account of truth. It is fortunate that to avoid the 'mob-rule' charge we have no need to appeal to a universal canon of rational inquiry. The coherence conditions on an absolute inquiry series are, as noted above, exceedingly strong, so strong that even the most ardent believer in the cunning of reason could scarcely suppose them to be possible outcomes of consensuses achieved through mob rule.

Other, and more insidious objections may be anticipated from metaphysical realist quarters. First, it may be argued that our account does not fully meet the prime requirement for an account of truth, that of so explicating truth as to reveal its unconditioned nature—its complete freedom from constraint by limits or contamination by error. What the account precludes, so the objection runs, is not conditioning by error and limitation, but rather certain kinds of apparent conditioning by error and limitation. In fact, the objector will insist, the conditions we have laid down are neither sufficient nor necessary for genuine freedom from error and limitation. For there may be sources of error that can never be recognized from the standpoint of any conceivable type of inquiry; and no matter how powerful the constraints that are imposed on an inquiry in terms of internal coherence of its products and their external coherence with the fruits of other inquiries, they will not ensure that what appears from the standpoint of that inquiry to be a source of error or limitation really is so. In response to this line of argument we can but voice the suspicion that, like the idea that there are truths which are inaccessible not just to all actual, but to all conceivable types of inquirers, so too the idea that there are sources of error and limitation unrecognizable from the standpoint of any conceivable type of inquiry rests upon the fantasy of an absolute standpoint, a world's-eye point of view.

At the 'theological' pole of pragmatist thought about truth lie accounts which, in attempting to do justice to truth's transcendence of error, limitation, and partiality, fail to relate it sufficiently to the historical fortunes of human inquiries.[6] Here belong attempts to ground the notion of truth in the notion of an ultimate and complete theory, in the notion of the fortunes of an inquiry conducted in perfect accordance with the canons of rationality, or in the notion of a consensus achieved under conditions absolutely free of distortion and coercion. At the 'secular' pole lie accounts which, in attempting to do full justice to truth's immanence in history, deny altogether its transcendence of the outcomes of finite inquiries. Here are to be found accounts that equate truth with currently attainable consensus or currently warranted assertibility.

In attempting to satisfy the conflicting demands of transcendence and immanence it may be thought that I have ended up too near the theological pole. If so, the attempt to defend the claim that science has shown an accumulation of truth is likely to fail. Even if the balance is right, the task is evidently a formidable one.

---

[6] These characterizations of the extremes of pragmatist thought derive from Ernan McMullin, in conversation.

IV

Scientific Absolutism: Historical Grounds

My concern in this chapter is to outline a defence of scientific absolutism by an appeal to the history of science. The account of truth that has been offered ties the notion of truth to that of an absolute inquiry series. The general strategy for defence of scientific absolutism would, therefore, be relatively straightforward were it possible to argue that human scientific inquiry has generated the initial segment of an absolute inquiry series. But that direct route is almost certainly not open to us. For an indefinitely protracted inquiry to yield an absolute inquiry series, the inquirers would have to possess an unlimited evidence-gathering capacity; and that we almost certainly do not have. If we are so to relate the outcomes of human inquiry to an absolute inquiry series as to vindicate scientific absolutism, then a more devious strategy must be contrived.

The indirect strategy to be pursued here is as follows. Let us call a sequence of consensuses generated by a human inquiry indefinitely prosecuted under circumstances optimal for inquiry 'an IHS'. First, it is argued by induction on the history of science that an IHS would show many of the features of an absolute inquiry series. Secondly, it is argued that possession of those features is sufficient to ensure that what is true from the standpoint of an IHS is true from the standpoint of an absolute inquiry series. Finally it is argued, again by induction on the history of science, that from the standpoint of an IHS the history of science shows an accumulation of truth.

In preparation for the first stage of this defence let us recapitulate the characteristics of an absolute inquiry series. They are as follows:

(i) Infinite transcendence of error: from the standpoint of the series there are no insuperable sources of systematic error;

(ii) Infinite resolution of questions: there are, from the standpoint of the series, no well-posed but indeterminable questions;

(iii) Absolute dominance: whenever there is an ultimate divergence between it and some other inquiry series, it dominates that other inquiry series by providing an explanation of the divergence in terms of error or limitation in the alien procedures of inquiry; but the relation is always an asymmetric one—no other inquiry series dominates an absolute inquiry series.

Evidently the second stage of the argument outlined above, that which is to show that what is true from the standpoint of an IHS is true from the standpoint of an absolute inquiry series, will be the less onerous the more closely IHSs can be shown to resemble absolute inquiry series. We have, however, already conceded one difference between IHSs and absolute inquiry series. The insuperable constraints on our evidence-gathering capacities impose limits on the ability of human inquiries to resolve singular questions, no matter how prolonged and how favourable the circumstances. For the moment I shall proceed optimistically, roughing out a case for the claim that an IHS would have all the characteristics of an absolute inquiry series save infinite capacity to resolve singular questions.

The cases to be made for infinite resolution of general questions, infinite transcendence of error, and absolute domination by an IHS rest on extrapolations from the history of science. Before presenting those cases it is as well to consider the general form of such extrapolations. Take infinite resolution of general questions. Our starting-point is the observation that from the standpoint of current theories we can see how general questions that have arisen at earlier stages in inquiry have been successively determined or dissolved at later stages. We are out to substantiate the claim that from the standpoint of an IHS there would be no irresoluble general questions. Simple extrapolation does not suffice here: what is needed is a double extrapolation. Consider sequences of histories of science told from the standpoints of temporally successive scientific consensuses, culminating in a history of science told from the standpoint of our science. Let us concentrate now on the chronicles of the resolution of general questions provided by successive histories in such a sequence. Clearly, just as later scientific consensuses may not only expand but also revise earlier ones, so later chronicles of the resolution of general questions will frequently revise as well as expand earlier ones.[1] Thus, for example, a sixteenth-century history of astronomy might well present as an instance of progress Copernicus' treatment of the problems of variation in amount of

---

[1] Cf. G. Bachelard's reflections on 'recurrent' history of scientific progress, continually retold in the light of new scientific consensuses: *L'activité rationaliste de la physique contemporaine*, Paris, 1951, ch. 1.

annual precession of the equinoxes and in the obliquity of the ecliptic. But a well-informed seventeenth-century history of astronomy would revise this assessment in the light of evidence accumulated by Tycho Brahe and others for the illusory nature of the supposed variations.[2] As a basis for the first stage of the required double extrapolation, it must be shown that substantial parts of the earlier chronicles of resolution of theoretical questions are preserved in later chronicles. On the basis of this generalization about the hypothetical history of the history of science, we may extrapolate to the conclusion that a substantial proportion of what appear from the standpoint of current theories to constitute resolutions of general questions would appear thus from the standpoint of an IHS. Only in the presence of this first extrapolation are we in a position to extrapolate from the initial premiss—the successive posing and resolving of general questions that is apparent from the standpoint of our theories—to the required conclusion—the infinite resolution of general questions by an IHS.

The same type of double extrapolation is needed if historical support is to be obtained for possession by an IHS of other features of an absolute inquiry series. In each case we must first, by extrapolation from a sequence of hypothetical histories of science, make a case for the existence of a substantial measure of conformity between the way the history of science appears from the standpoint of our theories and the way it would appear from the standpoint of an IHS. Only then can we proceed to extrapolate from the currently apparent achievements of our finite inquiries to the likely achievements of an indefinitely protracted inquiry. In the following discussion it is the second extrapolation that will be the focus of attention, for it is the one subject to the most salient objections.

'There *is* no such thing as a classification of the ways in which men may arrive at an error': thus Augustus de Morgan.[3] Certainly the rough categorizations of sources of error to be offered here and in subsequent chapters make no pretence at exhaustiveness or refinement. To start with we may distinguish affective from cognitive

[2] On Copernicus' explanation of these supposed phenomena see J. L. E. Dreyer, *A History of Astronomy from Thales to Kepler*, 2nd edn., New York, 1953, 329–30. Johannes Stadius praises Copernicus' account in the historical introduction to his *Tabulae Bergenses* of 1560. G. B. Riccioli, however, is more critical in his monumental treatise of 1651 on the history and current state of astronomy: *Almagestum novum astronomiam veterum novamque complectens*, Bologna, vol. 1, 165–9.

[3] *Formal Logic* (1847), ed. by A. E. Taylor, London, 1926, p. 276.

sources of error—'hot' and 'cold' sources in the engaging terminology of cognitive psychology. The former relate to persons' preferences, desires, and interests: here belong self-deception, wishful thinking, 'false consciousness', etc. The latter relate to persons' perceptual, imaginative, and ratiocinative capacities. Cognitive sources of error will be our main concern. Within the class of cognitive sources a rough and ready distinction will be drawn between, on the one hand, observational error, which affects the quality of the evidence that may be appealed to in order to resolve general questions and, on the other hand, methodological error, which concerns the ways in which evidence is deployed to resolve general questions. Observational error is a category of vast scope, including not only error arising from defects in and misapplication of the unaided senses, but also the whole spectrum of types of experimental error, from inept performance and misapplication of measurement procedures to misinterpretation of the readings of instruments arising from lack of theoretical understanding of their functioning. Methodological error too is a broad category, ranging from straightforward types such as commission of logical fallacies in working out the implications of evidence to more complex and context dependent errors such as inappropriate appeal to criteria of simplicity and inappropriate trade-off between different criteria for the resolution of theoretical conflict.

Transcendence of observational error includes the many cases in which, from the standpoint of our theories, we can make out successive refinements of measurement procedures through improvement in the design and calibration of instruments. Here too belong cases in which we can discern successive improvements in the quality of data that have accrued from better understanding of the conditions under which instruments function reliably. In the next chapter the relations between reduction of theories and transcendence of observational error are considered, and in Chapter VII ways in which to assess the reliabilities of measurement and observation procedures are discussed. Transcendence of observational error will emerge from those discussions as perhaps the least problematic of the categories of historical evidence to be marshalled in support of scientific absolutism.

Difficult and pressing questions arise in connection with transcendence of methodological error. How is this generic source of error to be broken down into specific sources of error? And how are the reliabilities of methods for the resolution of general questions in the light of evidence to be estimated from the standpoint of our current theories? Standard arguments suggest the futility of the quest for a universally applicable canon for the reliable resolution of theoretical questions; and certainly the history of science provides no support for a vision of methodological progress in which particular sources of error in the deployment of evidence have been overcome through cumulative articulation of and subsequent adherence to such generally applicable rules. Indeed, the very idea that particular generally binding rules for the handling of evidence may have been 'discovered' at particular dates has an air of absurdity.

I shall argue in due course that though the quest for a general *organon* is futile, the articulation of locally applicable criteria and the testing of their reliability is not only possible, but constitutes a routine component of scientific inquiry. Here are some modest examples of locally applicable rules, cast in the form of recipes for the avoidance of error. In each case a reason for holding the rule to be reliable is sketched. (i) In attempting to resolve questions about the effects of continental drift on plant distributions, do not attach much importance to present distributions of spore-bearing plants or of the smaller-seeded flowering plants. Reasons: there is direct evidence for aerial transport of spores; and recent theoretical study of transport of bodies in turbulent airstreams suggests that small seeds may be carried across oceans in trade winds in significant numbers over long time-spans.[4] (ii) In seeking phylogenetic explanations for morphological features of organisms, it is unwise to act on the assumption that each feature is adapted to specific aspects of the environment. Reason: certain features are likely to be by-products of the developmental processes that give rise to adaptive features.[5] In Chapters VII and VIII I shall consider in detail the various ways in which the reliability of methods for the assessment of hypotheses and theories may be established a posteriori, and I shall claim that such local rules can serve many of the purposes that have been supposed to demand a universal canon of reliable methods. The claim is a contentious one. For the moment,

[4] D. Mollison, 'Long distance wind dispersal of organisms' (forthcoming).
[5] Cf. S. J. Gould and R. C. Lewontin, 'The spandrels of San Marco and the Panglossian paradigm: a critique of the adaptationist programme', *Proceedings of the Royal Society, Series B*, 205 (1978), 581–98.

however, we shall rest content with the modest and uncontroversial claim that the history of science shows many cases of recognition and subsequent avoidance of local and theoretical context dependent methodological errors.

Experimental error may lead us to accept or reject a hypothesis on the basis of unsound evidence. Methodological error may lead us to accept or reject a hypothesis on the basis of an unsound use of the available evidence. Error in hypotheses and theories is often attributable, however, neither to unsound evidence nor to unsound use of the available evidence, but rather to insufficiency in the quantity or range of evidence. The sizes of past dinosaur populations are, to revert to our standard example, likely to remain forever inaccessible to us, as are precise details of past daily weather. Yet such evidence is obviously germane to a whole range of theoretical questions in population genetics, ecology, climatology, etc. We are here, it seems, forced to admit that certain specific theoretical questions are either irresoluble or resoluble only at the cost of committing the error of deciding questions on the basis of insufficient evidence. Both the hypothesis of infinite transcendence of error and the hypothesis of infinite resolution of general questions are thus called in question.

The overcoming of observational error is often, quite literally, a matter of elimination. Specks of dust are wiped from the eyepiece, air resistance is avoided by expelling the air, etc. As long as elimination is our model for overcoming sources of error and limitation in our inquiries, inaccessibility of evidence is apt to appear an insuperable obstacle. To 'eliminate' it one would have to gain access to evidence that is *ex hypothesi* inaccessible. But, of course, elimination is not the only mode of transcendence of error and limitation. As Galileo so famously showed, there are ways of discounting interfering factors other than literal removal. In the expression made famous by the first English translation of his *Two Chief World Systems*, we may 'defalcate the impediments of matter': to find out the weight of the goods we may estimate the weight of the packaging rather than unpack them; to confirm the parabolic trajectories of projectiles in a vacuum we may calculate the effects of air resistance rather than have to remove the air. In other words, we may overcome a source of error or limitation by compensating for it rather than removing it. Can we generally hope to compensate for the errors and limitations in our resolution of general questions that result from the inaccessibility of certain types of evidence?

We cannot, of course, hope to compensate at a stroke for all the diverse bodies of evidence that are at once germane to outstanding general questions and utterly inaccessible to us; nor do the hypotheses of infinite transcendence of error and infinite resolution of general questions by an indefinitely protracted human scientific inquiry require us to do so. Rather we need to substantiate the claim that whenever entirely inaccessible evidence of some particular type appears to be indispensable for the reliable resolution of a general question, some other reliable way of resolving the issue would in due course be discovered were inquiry to proceed for long enough under favourable circumstances. Let us call this 'the evidential compensation thesis'.

What aspects of the history of science can be adduced in support of the evidential compensation thesis? Direct support arises from instances in which questions whose resolution at first seemed to be blocked by the complete inaccessibility of evidence of some particular kind have subsequently been reliably settled by other means. Consider non-woody plants. Unlike, say, woody plants and vertebrate animals they have a very sparse fossil record, and questions about the precise ancestry of extant species appeared until the 1930s to be for the most part unanswerable. However, it turned out that on occasion reliable information about ancestry could be obtained despite the absence of a fossil record. For so-called 'allopolyploid' species are derived by interspecific hybridization followed by a process of chromosome reduplication that restores fertility. The ancestry of allopolyploids can, in certain cases, be confirmed by their experimental synthesis.[6] Or consider the question of the occurrence of continental drift. Until the 1960s it could reasonably be argued that the available types of evidence, geological, geophysical and biogeographical, were inconclusive and open to alternative interpretation. But study of magnetic anomalies on the ocean floor has now yielded a firm resolution of the issue.[7] Indirect inductive support for the evidential compensation thesis accrues from cases in which the reliable

---

[6] See, e.g., D. Briggs and S. M. Walters, *Plant Variation and Evolution*, 2nd rev. edn., Cambridge, 1984, ch. 11.

[7] See, e.g., A. Hallam, *A Revolution in the Earth Sciences. From Continental Drift to Plate Tectonics*, Oxford, 1973.

resolution of general questions has been overdetermined by distinct bodies of evidence.[8] A striking example is provided by the concurrence of estimates of Avogadro's number on the basis of distinct types of evidence, a concurrence that was famously presented by Jean Perrin as proof of the reality of atoms and molecules.[9]

There is a serious objection to this attempt to establish the evidential compensation thesis by induction on the history of science. Each of the cases of evidential compensation and evidential overdetermination mentioned above has arisen within some particular theoretical framework. Thus the issue of continental drift was posed and resolved against a substantial and diverse background of geophysical theory; the issue of allopolypoid speciation of plants arose in the context of experimental and theoretical genetics and cytology; and the independent techniques of estimation of Avogadro's number all presupposed a molecular kinetic theory. However, so the objection runs, once we turn from such local issues to questions which concern the adequacy of entire theories or world-pictures, the defence of the evidential compensation breaks down. Whereas within a theoretical framework it may well be that specific issues are generally overdetermined with respect to distinct types of evidence, at the level of entire theories the evidential compensation thesis is implausible: here underdetermination by evidence is the norm.

A full response to this objection must wait on the discussion of underdetermination of theory by evidence. But it is worth anticipating briefly the part of the discussion of underdetermination that concerns the history of science. There is a widely prevalent view of the history of science that may be called 'catastrophism'. The catastrophist image is one in which scientific development has involved wholesale confrontation of entire all-encompassing world-pictures: Stoic vs. Aristotelian cosmology, corpuscular-mechanism vs. scholastic natural philosophy, the quantum-physical world-

---

[8] Many examples of concurrence of hypotheses based on different bodies of evidence are retailed by D. Lamb and S. M. Easton, *Multiple Discovery. The Pattern of Scientific Progress*, Trowbridge, 1984; see also W. F. Ogburn and D. S. Thomas, 'Are innovations inevitable?', *Political Science Quarterly*, 37 (1922), 83–98.

[9] See *Les atomes*, Paris, 1913, 293–5, where Perrin tabulates the congruent values got by thirteen independent methods. On Perrin's determinations of Avogadro's number see M. J. Nye, *Molecular Reality: A Perspective on the Scientific Work of Jean Perrin*, London, 1972, especially pp. 130–6, 160–1.

picture vs. the world-picture of classical physics. If the history of science really has shown a sequence of such epic confrontations, then the evidential compensation thesis is surely in serious trouble. In Chapter VI I suggest that even the most dramatic paradigm shifts have come about not through single global confrontations and resolutions, but rather through multiple local confrontations and resolutions in the various domains of inquiry governed by the conflicting paradigms.

The evidential compensation thesis—the claim that whenever a body of entirely inaccessible evidence appears to be indispensable for the resolution of a general question, sufficiently prolonged further investigation would reveal an alternative means of reliable resolution—is a very strong thesis. Consider the analogous but more general claim that no particular kind of evidence is indispensable for the reliable resolution of any general question. This more general claim is grossly implausible. Consider such kinds of evidence as 'evidence of the internal anatomy of organisms' or 'evidence relating to the interactions of particles at very high energies'. Were such bodies of evidence to be completely inaccessible to us, vast numbers of general questions, the topics of entire disciplines, would be irresoluble. So the evidential compensation thesis involves a strong claim about our evidence-gathering capacities. It implies that our senses, the extensions of them potentially available to us through construction of instruments, and our actual and physically possible situations in the universe, are such that none of the indispensable kinds of evidence is entirely unavailable to us. (In Chapter VI it is, indeed, conceded that certain special types of questions may be irresoluble due to inaccessibility of indispensable evidence; and in Chapter IX an attempt is made to repair the damage to the case for scientific absolutism that arises from this concession.)

Let us concentrate now on the second of the characteristics of an absolute inquiry series listed above, infinite resolution of questions. It has already been noted that given the inevitable limitations on human evidence-gathering capacities no IHS can be expected to manifest infinite resolution of singular questions. But to the extent that the evidential compensation thesis just mooted holds good, this limitation is not fatal to the claim that an IHS would show infinite resolution of general scientific questions.

In his once notorious *Die sieben Welträtsel* ('The Seven World-

Riddles') the physiologist Emil Du Bois-Reymond set out seven enigmas.[10] Three of them were, so he claimed, utterly insoluble: the nature of the fundamental notions of physics, matter, and force; the origin of motion; and the bases of sensation and reflexive consciousness. Three he held to be so difficult as to be likely to resist solution for the indefinite future: the origin of life; the reasons for adaptation of organisms to their environments; and the genesis of reasoning and language. Concerning the question of the freedom of will, he was unsure whether to assign it to the category of utterly insoluble transcendental questions or to the category of those very unlikely to be resolved. Writing in 1899 Ernst Haeckel, the leading German protagonist of organic evolution, claimed to be able to offer at least the outlines of resolutions of six of the riddles.[11] The seventh, the problem of free will, he dismissed as ill posed.

Du Bois-Reymond's enigmas illustrate well the diversity of types of challenges to the infinite resolution of general questions by an IHS. In the case of the explanation of organisms' adaptations to their environments the apparent obstacle was, for Du Bois-Reymond, the lack of any suitable explanatory theory. Haeckel met this challenge by indicating how an evolutionary theory could provide the required explanations. In the case of the origin of life Du Bois-Reymond's reservations concerned the difficulty of understanding how the dynamic equilibria characteristic of life arose by the interactions of atoms in accordance with the laws of physics.[12] Today doubts of this sort would be more likely to focus on the utter inaccessibility of evidence about terrestrial states of affairs in the remote pre-Cambrian era in which life is thought to have originated on earth. A latter-day Haeckel might well seek to allay such

[10] This work was written in response to the extensive debate sparked off by his address to the Berlin Academy of Sciences in 1872, in which he had argued that the questions of the explanation of consciousness and of the connection between matter and force reveal absolute limits to human knowledge (*Ueber die Grenzen des Naturerkennens*, Leipzig, 1872).

[11] *Die Welträtsel*, Bonn, 1899; trans. J. McCabe, *The Riddle of the Universe*, London, 1900. Haeckel did not claim the possibility of outright resolution of the riddles but rather that each could be analysed into, on the one hand, a soluble question about the attributes and evolution of 'substance' and, on the other hand, the enigma of the nature of substance itself. On Haeckel's criticisms of Du Bois-Reymond see N. Rescher, *The Limits of Science*, Berkeley, 1984, 115 ff.

[12] Cf. H. Hensel, 'Emil Du Bois-Reymond, der Schüler Johannes Müllers, seine Stellung zum Vitalismus und zur materialistischen Philosophie', in G. Mann, ed., *Naturwissen und Erkenntnis im 19. Jahrhundert: Emil Du Bois-Reymond*, Hildesheim, 1981, 27–44.

scepticism by drawing attention to successful syntheses of organic
macromolecules under circumstances designed to simulate the
'primeval soup' and by suggesting that research along these lines
may eventually compensate for the lack of direct evidence about the
earliest terrestrial environments.

Current scientific theories may make one sanguine about the
prospects for resolving questions about the origin of life and the
reasons for biological adaptations. In the case of Du Bois-
Reymond's enigmas of the origin of motion and the nature of the
fundamental notions of physics, matter, and force, it is perhaps
arguable from the standpoint of current theories that the questions
are ill posed, however well posed they may have seemed within his
strictly mechanistic world-picture.[13]

We have seen that four of Du Bois-Reymond's enigmas, the ones
that would generally be regarded as scientific, no longer appear
entirely insoluble. The remaining enigmas concern topics that are
thought by some to remain problematic for reasons that have little
to do with the normal predicaments of scientific inquiry, dearth of
relevant evidence, and lack of explanatory theories. Thus it may be
argued that sentience is a genuinely enigmatic topic because it gives
rise to questions—Are bats sentient? If so, what is it like to be
one?—that are at once well posed and such that we cannot hope to
resolve them because we have no conception of evidence relevant to
them. (Such questions may appear to gainsay the dependence
postulated earlier between the well-posedness of a question according to a theory and its susceptibility to evidential considerations
given that theory.) It may be argued that the topics of reflexive
consciousness and freedom of the will are enigmatic not because we
are faced with determinate questions that we have no inkling how to
answer, but rather because we are unable even to pose the specific
questions whose resolution would dispel our bafflement and
unease. And it may be suggested that the genesis of reasoning and
language is enigmatic because it concerns preconditions for the
development of science: for it has often been thought that difficulties of principle are attendant on the attempt to achieve scientific
knowledge of the conditions of emergence and growth of scientific
knowledge itself.

---

[13] On Du Bois-Reymond's determinism and materialism see R. Malter,
' "Kausalitätstrieb" und Erkenntnisschranke. Zur philosophischen Grundposition
Emil Du Bois-Reymonds', in Mann, ed., *Naturwissen und Erkenntnis*, 45–77.

Such 'philosophical' challenges to the infinite resolution hypothesis are further discussed in Chapter IX. With regard to scientific challenges which maintain the insolubility of particular questions on the grounds of the inaccessibility of apparently indispensable data, a stand has already been taken. With regard to scientific challenges which maintain the insolubility of certain questions on the grounds of our inability to come up with appropriate explanatory theories and hypotheses, a stand can be taken forthwith. The history of science is well stocked with examples of questions once thought on such grounds to be entirely intractable, but from the standpoint of current theories either resolved or well on the way to resolution; sufficiently well stocked in fact to suggest by extrapolation that such challenges are ineffective.

Defence of the claim that an IHS would show infinite transcendence of error and infinite resolution of general questions faces, as we have just seen, many difficulties. But in conducting the defence it is quite clear where in the history of human inquiry the relevant evidence is to be sought: namely, in the lines of inquiry that are ancestral to present scientific consensuses. When we turn to the third of the features of an absolute inquiry series, absolute domination, however, it is far from clear where, if anywhere, in the history of human inquiry we can hope to find the requisite evidence. Indeed, it appears initially to be quite implausible that such evidence is to be had. The claim that an IHS would show absolute domination with respect to general questions is a claim about the relations between the fruits of an indefinitely protracted human scientific inquiry and the fruits of all other possible types of inquiry. Given that these possible types of inquiry may include ones conducted by beings whose sensory and ratiocinative equipments are not only profoundly different from, but also far more powerful than our own, it is hard to see how any appeal to the history of human inquiry could substantiate the claim. Superadded to this is a problem about standpoints. Absolute domination is defined not only in terms of the ways other inquiry series appear from the standpoint of a given inquiry series, but also in terms of the ways in which the given inquiry series appears from the standpoints of other inquiry series. How can we hope to adduce evidence from within the history of human scientific inquiry for the ways in which the fruits of that inquiry would appear from the standpoints of non-human scientific inquiries?

The general strategy will be to offer certain relations that have held between the fruits of different traditions of human inquiry as a model for the relations that would hold between an IHS and the fruits of other possible inquiries. As we shall see, the key to effective engagement with the difficulties is a rejection of the view of the history of science as constituted by a single tradition of inquiry culminating in our science. When the history of science is viewed with more discernment as constituted by a plurality of variously interacting traditions of inquiry, the difficulties can be overcome.

With apologies for the introduction of yet more terminology, let us consider in the most schematic of terms certain possible outcomes of an encounter between divergent traditions of inquiry I and I'. When continued inquiry in I leads to resolution of the divergences in favour of I', we have *assimilation* of I' by I. When continued inquiry in I generates an explanation for the divergencies in terms of error or inadequacy in I', we have *domination of I' by I*. When I eventually resolves all its divergences from I' by assimilation, domination, or some combination of the two, we say that I is *resilient* in the face of I'.

Using the terminology we may express the claim that an IHS would show absolute dominance in terms of the outcomes of hypothetical future encounters with the fruits of non-human inquiries. Absolute dominance by an IHS is equivalent to the claim that the eventual outcome of each such hypothetical encounter would satisfy the following conditions:

(i) *Resilience*—the human inquiry would show resilience in the face of the alien inquiry;

(ii) *Indomitability*—the human inquiry would not be dominated by the alien inquiry.

Let us now consider the types of historical evidence that may be adduced in support of the claim that an IHS would satisfy the resilience and indomitability conditions.

In approaching the resilience condition it is instructive to consider first a tempting but defective extrapolation from the history of science. On this approach one would start by considering the tradition of inquiry that has given rise to our science. One would then consider the cases in which that tradition has encountered the fruits of wholly or partially independent traditions of inquiry. Next, one would seek to show that in each such case our tradition of scientific inquiry has shown resilience in the face of the other tradition. Finally, it would be argued that the encounters between our tradition of scientific inquiry and these other human traditions of inquiry provide a model for hypothetical future encounters with the fruits of alien inquiries. Just as our tradition of scientific inquiry has proved resilient in the face of all other enquiries, so an indefinitely prolonged human scientific inquiry would prove resilient come what may in the way of alien inquiries. This strategy is defective on two counts. The idea that our science has been generated by a single tradition of inquiry is obviously untenable if we consider the entire span of the history of science from classical antiquity; and, as already noted, it has become increasingly evident to historians of science that it remains untenable even if we confine our attention to the modern period. Rather, our science is to be seen as having emerged from the interactions of a multiplicity of traditions of inquiry, some of them not by any stretch of our conception of science scientific in orientation. Secondly, this approach is one that can yield evidence only of the resilience of scientific inquiry through domination of other inquiries. If we insist on considering our science as the product of a single tradition of inquiry, we cannot coherently suppose that tradition to have assimilated substantial bodies of material from other traditions of inquiry: for then those other traditions of inquiry would have to be accounted part of the scientific tradition. Only the most arrant of human-species chauvinists could imagine that it would be through dominance alone that an indefinitely prolonged human inquiry would prove resilient in the face of other inquiries: for that is tantamount to assuming that we are, cognitively speaking, by so far the best of which the universe is capable that we would have nothing to learn from any other physically possible type of inquirers.

The failure of this crude approach is instructive. To make a case for satisfaction of the resilience condition by an indefinitely pro-longed human inquiry we must consider evidence of the capacity of traditions of inquiry to assimilate material from other traditions, as well as evidence of their capacity to dominate them. And to do justice to the history of science we must consider our science as the product not of a single tradition of inquiry, but rather a multiplicity of variously interacting traditions.

As an alternative approach I suggest that the relations of traditions of inquiry ancestral to our science both to each other and to non-ancestral traditions be considered as models for the relations that would hold between an indefinitely prolonged human inquiry and alien inquiries. Thus we may hope to find evidence of resilience by the ancestral traditions manifested both by their assimilation of material from other traditions and by their domination of other traditions. Given such evidence we may then extrapolate to the conclusion that an indefinitely prolonged human inquiry would satisfy the resilience condition, whilst taking due account of the likelihood that such resilience would involve extensive learning from alien inquirers.

Detailed consideration of the ways in which traditions and subtraditions of inquiry may be individuated and of the diverse ways in which they may interact lies far beyond the scope of this work. But a few points about individuation of traditions require mention. In much recent writing in the history of science shared belief provides the chief basis for differentiation of traditions, secondary roles being played by questions of participation, institutional basis, and flow of information. Indeed, there is often room for the suspicion that the units about which historical narrative is woven are just the much criticized 'isms' of bad old-fashioned history of ideas—mechanism, vitalism, Newtonianism, Darwinism, etc.—in fashionable disguises: the mechanistic *Weltanschauung*, the vitalist paradigm, the Newtonian research tradition, etc. If substantial assimilation of beliefs from one tradition into another is to be conceptually on the cards, it is important that the definition of a tradition of inquiry should not require a high degree of doxastic homogeneity and continuity.

Given that we are aiming at a conclusion about relations between our inquiries and the hypothetical inquiries of alien beings, it is clearly the more extremely differentiated traditions of human inquiry that will be of primary interest. Perhaps the most obvious dimension of differentiation is that of cultural context. On this score pride of place must surely go to the traditions of inquiry in medicine, cosmology, alchemy, etc., that arose in the Far East on the one hand and in Europe, the Near, and the Middle East on the other, traditions of inquiry which combined a very high degree of disparity in cultural context with almost complete isolation for at least a millennium. Within these major traditions it is, of course, possible to distinguish in certain fields partially independent traditions of inquiry—Korean and Chinese cosmology; Indian, Assyrian, and Greek astronomy, etc. And at yet lower degrees of autonomy one may distinguish traditions of inquiry that have some limited degree of national and/or institutional independence—the Newtonian and Cartesian programmes in celestial dynamics, the Galtonian and Mendelian programmes in the study of heredity, for example.

Differentiation in cultural context is not the only kind of differentiation that is of interest to us. Alien intelligences may be expected to differ from us not only in the social organization of their inquiries, but also in their cognitive interests. On this score interactions of traditions of inquiry which differ widely in the motives with which they approach a given subject matter may be of interest. Consider the medieval and Renaissance 'philosophical' tradition of inquiry into celestial matters, a tradition concerned with kinds of motions and substances, as opposed to the coeval 'mathematical' tradition of inquiry into celestial matters, a tradition largely concerned with accurate prediction of apparent celestial positions;[14] or consider pre-Darwinian studies of the structure of organisms motivated by interest in the manifestations of Divine Providence in nature as opposed to those motivated by a descriptive comparative anatomical interest.[15] Similarly, alien intelligences may be expected to differ from us in their sensory equipment, and hence in the kinds of data available to them. On this score traditions of inquiry that are strongly differentiated with respect to the types of evidence they bring to bear on a particular subject matter are of interest: consider, for example, the biogeographical tradition of speculation about past dispositions of land and sea on the basis of the distributions of types of organisms, on the one hand, and the tradition of speculation on the basis of geological and geophysical data, on the other.[16]

Cases of resilience of traditions of inquiry through domination of other traditions of inquiry are more readily documented from the history of science than are cases of their resilience through assimilation. In part this is for a reason already mentioned: namely, that

[14] On the two disciplinary contexts for the study of the heavens see, e.g., N. Jardine, 'The significance of the Copernican orbs', *Journal of the History of Astronomy*, 12 (1982), 168–94.

[15] On pre-Darwinian concern with the providential design of organisms see M. Mandelbaum, 'The scientific background to evolutionary theory in biology', *Journal of the History of Ideas*, 18 (1957), 342–61.

[16] See H. Frankel, 'The palaeobiogeological debate over the problem of disjunctively distributed life forms', *Studies in History and Philosophy of Science*, 12 (1981), 211–59.

historians often individuate research traditions mainly in terms of extent of shared belief, and that thus individuated one research tradition cannot coherently be supposed to assimilate a substantial body of material from a divergent tradition. In part this imbalance arises from the understandable prevalence (even amongst recent historians of science with a healthy awareness of the dangers of 'presentist' interpretation and assessment) of concentration on disciplines that prefigure our disciplines of scientific inquiry and on the genesis of hypotheses and theories that adumbrate or anticipate our own. Of course, a substantial minority of recent history of science has been concerned with traditions of inquiry that would be excluded by such retrospective criteria. But even here a kind of second-order presentism is often displayed, little attention being paid to the careers of such traditions of inquiry after their initial confrontation with 'mainstream' science. Thus it is that we have detailed studies of Paduan natural philosophy in the century prior to Galileo's departure from the city, but relatively little on its career in the following century.[17] Similarly, the history of astrology has been widely studied for the period before 1700, but there is much less serious study for the period following its supposed death at the hands of 'the new science'.[18] There is a similarly marked imbalance of scholarship in the case of Chinese science and technology before and after the arrival of Jesuit mathematicians in Peking in the early seventeenth century.

Evidence of domination by traditions of inquiry ancestral to present scientific consensus is most readily adduced where divergent traditions of inquiry were once in live confrontation with them. Take, by way of stock examples, the conflict between Galilean mathematical science and Aristotelian natural philosophy or the conflict between the Galtonian and Mendelian research programmes in genetics. In each case the standard historical accounts not only tell us of the issues on which the protagonists of the rival traditions saw themselves as being at odds, but also of the

[17] On the reception and assimilation of Galilean doctrines in Italy see M. L. Soppelsa, *Genesi del metodo galileiano e tramonto dell'aristotelismo nella Scuola di Padova*, Padua, 1974; M. Torrini, *Dopo Galileo. Una polemica scientifica (1684–1711)*, Florence, 1979.

[18] P. Curry has documented the assimilation of astrological themes into 'orthodox' natural philosophy and the various attempts to make astrology scientifically respectable in England in this later period: 'The Decline of Astrology in Early Modern England', forthcoming Ph.D. thesis, University of London.

ways in which protagonists of the 'victorious' tradition explained their divergences from the 'vanquished' tradition in terms of error in their opponents' procedures of inquiry. The task of exhibiting the resilience of traditions of inquiry ancestral to our science through domination of other traditions has in such cases already been performed for us at least in part by the original actors.

More problematic, though for our purposes of great importance, are the relatively few cases where the traditions of inquiry ancestral to our science have encountered really substantially divergent traditions—encounters of which perhaps the most striking is that between European and Chinese science and technology in the seventeenth century. In such cases it is highly questionable whether there was active contention: here there is little question of the original protagonists of the 'victorious' traditions having set out arguments for the dominance by their own traditions of the alien traditions.

Faced with classical Chinese astronomy, cosmology, alchemy, and medicine a likely initial impression is that of an almost complete lack of congruence with Western science at the level of explanatory principles and general theory. Such wholesale disparity is apt to make the task of exhibiting the dominance of Western traditions of inquiry appear unfeasible. When we turn to low-level beliefs about regularities in observed phenomena, however, substantial coincidences becomes apparent in a whole variety of fields.[19] We find, for example, remarkable concurrences in beliefs about the periodicities of celestial phenomena, in beliefs about the relative locations of light sources, shading, and intervening bodies, and in beliefs about the effects of administration of various herbal preparations. And the range of congruent beliefs is greatly extended when we turn our attention from those of which we have written records to those that can be reliably inferred from classical Chinese technology. Once this background of low-level concurrences is filled in, the attempt to show the dominance of 'Western science' ceases to appear so daunting. We may hope to explain certain of the more modest divergences in terms similar to those that are used to establish the dominance of one tradition over

---

[19] The following inexpert remarks are based on readings of the first two chapters of C. A. Ronan, *The Shorter Science and Civilisation in China: an Abridgement of Joseph Needham's Original Text*, Cambridge, 1968, vol. 1, and of S. Nakayama and N. Sivin, eds., *Chinese Science: Explorations of an Ancient Tradition*, Cambridge, Mass., 1973.

another within the Western scientific tradition. Thus many of the discrepancies between classical Chinese and Western positional astronomy can be explained in terms of such factors as the limited range of geographical standpoints from which observations were made, the limited accuracies of their instruments, the failure to develop systematic corrections for the effects of refraction at low celestial altitudes, etc. At the higher levels of cosmological theory divergences may perhaps be explained by appeal to such factors as the constraints imposed by subscription to Taoist cosmological principles, the lack of concern with questions of empirical adequacy, and the prevalence of strongly Sinocentric conceptions of the cosmos. Historically unilluminating though such explanations may be, they are grist to our somewhat eccentric mill.

Studies of assimilation, often in the form of tracing textual sources, mainly enter into standard historiography of science when the assimilating tradition is one that subsequently yielded what were, by our lights, major new contributions to science. To this category belong, for example, studies of the assimilation of the fruits of medieval Arab science into European traditions of inquiry in the later medieval and Renaissance periods. Dealing with assimilation on a smaller scale, we find, for example, studies of the incorporation of the fruits of the Newtonian research tradition in chemistry into the mainstream of chemical inquiry around the turn of the eighteenth century,[20] and studies of the assimilation in the course of the nineteenth century of aspects of phrenology into the mainstreams of anatomical and neurophysiological study of cerebral function and localization.[21] Such studies provide evidence of resilience by traditions of inquiry ancestral to our science through assimilation of material from other traditions.

Let us consider now the indomitability condition, the second condition for absolute dominance with regard to general questions. Negative evidence is needed to support the claim that an indefinitely prolonged human inquiry would satisfy the indomitability condition. It must be shown that there are no cases in which a tradition of inquiry not ancestral to our science has dominated traditions of inquiry that are ancestral to our science.

Attempts to confirm negative existential hypotheses are

[20] See A. Thackray, *Atoms and Powers*, Cambridge, Mass., 1970, chs. 7 and 8.
[21] See R. M. Young, *Mind, Brain and Adaptation in the Nineteenth Century: Cerebral Localization and its Biological Context from Gall to Ferrier*, Oxford, 1970.

generally problematic; and this particular attempt is beset by further specific difficulties. First, there is a difficulty about the interpretive standpoint. It may be objected that evidence of the required sort is inaccessible to us, because we are so conditioned by our scientific heritage as to be unable to understand how the traditions of inquiry ancestral to our science may have appeared from the standpoints of other traditions of inquiry. In particular, it may be urged that our standpoint debars us from appreciation of the grounds on which protagonists of alien traditions of inquiry may hold (or have held) the inquiries that have led to our science to be misguided or in error. A second major difficulty concerns the types of traditions of inquiry that could in principle yield evidence of the required sort. For it to be even on the cards that a tradition of inquiry should dominate another it is surely necessary that it be associated with an account of the ways in which inquiry itself is properly conducted. Should it turn out that such 'epistemologies' have arisen only in the context of traditions of inquiry ancestral to our science, then the failure of other traditions to dominate them is guaranteed in advance. But that failure will scarcely be relevant to the indomitability of an indefinitely prolonged human inquiry; unless we presumptuously assume ourselves to be the only beings capable of reflecting on the nature of inquiry itself. A final difficulty arises from the dearth of relevant historical studies. The required negative evidence is to be sought by examining traditions of inquiry that, having developed independently, have survived contact with the traditions of inquiry ancestral to our science: Chinese medicine in the last 300 years, for example. It may also be sought through the study of traditions of inquiry that have broken away from the 'mainstream' of scientific development: Paracelsian chemistry after 1700, post-Newtonian astrology, etc. As already noted, such studies are rare.

The first of these difficulties raises large questions about the possibility of understanding alien systems of belief. Certainly it is not generally true that disbelief in the premisses of a proposed explanation prevents the disbeliever from seeing that for those who do believe its premisses it constitutes a valid explanation. The onus is, then, on the objector to show that there is some special feature of explanations that impute systematic error to an interpreter (or to his intellectual ancestors) that renders such explanations opaque to his understanding.

The second alleged dificulty is, I suggest, spurious. Take the Paracelsian tradition of inquiry: this certainly involved an account of man's place in nature and of the modes of human acquisition of knowledge; and the same is true of the European traditions of inquiry in astrology and natural magic.[22]

The third difficulty must, of course, be conceded. But its implications should not be exaggerated. Though scholarly studies of the requisite type are still few and far between, it would be extraordinary were historians and anthropologists to have entirely overlooked traditions of inquiry that have given rise to systematic error-imputing explanations of their divergences from traditions of inquiry ancestral to our science. Such 'presumption' would surely have attracted attention!

If the history of human inquiry could be shown to yield the evidence required for the various extrapolations outlined, then the first stage of our general strategy for the defence of scientific absolutism would be completed. A case would have been made for the bold claim that were human inquiry indefinitely prolonged under sufficiently favourable circumstances an inquiry series would be generated that had all the characteristics of an absolute inquiry series, save that of unlimited capacity to resolve singular questions.

The next stage in our defensive strategy is, it may be remembered, to make out a case for the hypothesis that what are, from the standpoint of an IHS, true answers to general questions, are also true from the standpoint of an absolute inquiry series, that is are true *simpliciter*.

This second stage of the defence is relatively straightforward. Appealing as in the last chapter to the fiction of time-travel, imagine an indefinitely prolonged human inquiry in which, *per impossibile*, our evidence-gathering capacities are entirely unrestricted. Let us call the sequence of consensuses generated by such an inquiry an IHS*. An IHS* will have the characteristics of an IHS plus the crucial feature that sets IHSs apart from absolute inquiry series,

---

[22] On the Paracelsian world-picture see: K. Goldammer, *Paracelsus: Natur und Offenbarung*, Hanover, 1953; W. Pagel, *Paracelsus: an Introduction to Philosophical Medicine in the Era of the Renaissance*, Basel, 1958. On Renaissance astrological conceptions of the universe and man's place in it see E. Garin, *Lo zodiaco della vita*, Bari, 1976, trans. C. Jackson *et al.*, *Astrology in the Renaissance*, London, 1983. On Renaissance accounts of the acquisition of knowledge and power through natural magic see D. P. Walker, *Spiritual and Demonic Magic. From Ficino to Campanella*, London, 1958.

namely, an infinite capacity to resolve singular factual questions. So if our claims about the character of an IHS are correct, then an IHS* will be an absolute inquiry series. But it has been argued that our resolutions of general questions are, in the long run, unaffected by the limits on our power to resolve singular factual questions. So the move from an IHS to an IHS* does not affect the resolutions of general questions.[23] Generalizations true from the standpoint of an IHS are true from the standpoint of an IHS*; and since an IHS* is, so we have argued, an absolute inquiry series, they are true *simpliciter*.

As the third and final stage of our defence we must make out a case for supposing that, from the standpoint of an IHS, the history of science shows an accumulation of general truths. Again, the materials for the argument have already been assembled, this time in the course of our case for the infinite resolution of general questions by an IHS. Part of that case was an argument by induction on the ways in which the history of science appeared from the standpoints of successive scientific consensuses. The conclusion was that part at least of the cumulative resolution of theoretical questions that is apparent from the standpoint of our theories would also be apparent from the standpoint of an IHS.

Putting the outcomes of the last two phases of our argument together, the desired conclusion is reached. From the standpoint of an IHS the history of science shows an accumulation of general truths; what is true from the standpoint of an IHS is true: *ergo*, the history of science shows an accumulation of general truths.

It will not have escaped the reader's notice that this preliminary defence of scientific absolutism has deferred a whole series of major problems. To set the stage for the rest of this work let us briefly review the more pressing of them.

Perhaps the most direct threat to our case for scientific absolutism is that posed by strong versions of the thesis of underdetermination of theory by data, versions which imply the existence of non-trivially divergent theories such that no matter how prolonged, thorough, and determined our quest for evidence we could not achieve a reliable resolution of the issue between them. This is directly incompatible with the claim that an indefinitely prolonged

---

[23] In due course we shall concede that the claim may be too strong. This stage of the argument for scientific absolutism will be modified accordingly: see below, pp. 88–9 and 128.

human inquiry would have a potentially unlimited capacity to resolve general questions; and it is also at odds with the evidential compensation thesis, to which we appealed in defending the claim that such an inquiry would achieve infinite transcendence of error. In Chapters VI–VIII an attempt is made to disarm this menace. Certain purported examples of the thesis are rebutted; and it is suggested that, though globally applicable rules for the reliable resolution of theoretical conflict in the light of evidence are not to be had, we can expect in the long run to be able to resolve whatever theoretical conflicts we may encounter by appeal to local and context-dependent criteria. To complete the counter to the under-determination thesis I explore the question of the ways in which we may marshall evidence for the reliabilities of methods for the assessment of theories.

In discussing Du Bois-Reymond's world-riddles it was noted that the claim that human inquiry shows a potentially unlimited capacity to resolve general questions is subject not only to straightforwardly 'scientific' objections, but also to a variety of 'philosophical' objections. Such challenges form the subject matter of Chapter IX.

A third major menace to scientific absolutism concerns inter-theoretic interpretation. Our case for scientific absolutism rests on two claims about the cumulative nature of the history of science: the claim that it has shown cumulative resolution of general questions and the claim that it has shown progressive transcendence of error. These claims have been defended by appeal to historical evidence; but the validity of that evidence is itself called in question by the thesis of incommensurability of radically divergent theories and by the thesis of indeterminacy of intertheoretic interpretation. These theses are, in a sense, contraries: the former entails the non-existence of adequate schemes of intertheoretic interpretation; the latter entails the existence of many divergent equally adequate schemes. But though opposed, the theses similarly undermine the historical evidence for cumulative resolution of questions and progressive transcendence of error, given that all such evidence derives from translation and explication of past theories. In the next chapter it is argued that the threat is ineffective when one theory can be shown to be reducible to another. The notion of reduction introduced will be a broad one; broad enough to allow a very strong case for the prevalence of intertheoretic reduction in the history of science. It will be shown that from the standpoint of current theories reducibility of past theories entails resolution of theoretical questions and, in typical cases, transcendence of error as well. Thus a significant part of the evidence needed to sustain scientific absolutism will be defended against the threats posed by incommensurability and indeterminacy of interpretation.

V

Reduction and Interpretation

THE main aim of this chapter is to defend an important part of the historical evidence for scientific absolutism against the threats posed by incommensurability of theories and indeterminacy of interpretation. I offer first an account of the relation of reducibility between theories,[1] and go on to argue that the following hold.

(1) Reduction has been widely prevalent in the history of science.

(2) When past theories are reducible to current theories, then from the standpoint of the current theories cumulative resolution of questions has occurred and, in typical instances, transcendence of error as well.

(3) When a sound case for reduction of a past theory to a current one can be made, that case is vulnerable neither on the score of incommensurability of theories nor on the score of indeterminacy of intertheoretic interpretation.

The account of reduction to be proposed may be stated informally as follows. Theory T' is reducible to theory T just in case, from the standpoint of T and associated background theories, T' is empirically equivalent to a part of T over the range of evidence available to protagonists of T'.

First we must clarify the notion of empirical equivalence over a range of evidence. The 'items of evidence' to be appealed to are individual (token) experimental reports, reports of the values of parameters of objects or systems determined by the application of measurement procedures. The question of the conditions for confirmation or disconfirmation of a theory by an experimental report will be considered only in the context of background theories, from the standpoints of which questions of accuracy and range of measurement instruments and adequacy of performance of measurement procedures are judged.[2]

---

[1] Here, as subsequently, the theories at issue are scientific theories in the usual sense of the term, not the entire world-pictures that figured in Chapter III.

[2] The following tentative and incomplete treatment is quite close to the account of confirmation and disconfirmation given by C. Glymour in his *Theory and Evidence*, Princeton, 1980.

Let *e* be an experimental report of the outcome of adequately performed measurements on a sequence of parameters of an object or system *o*. Given a calibration of the instruments employed, it will in general be possible to infer from the values of parameters reported in *e* bounds on the values of those parameters possessed by *o*. Let *T* be the set of background theories involved in calibration of measurement instruments and in assessment of the adequacy of performances of measurement procedures. We say that an assignment of values to the parameters that figure in *e* is within the *T*-tolerance of *e* just in case:

(i) the measurement procedures whose outcomes *e* reports were, as judged from the standpoint of *T*, adequate;

(ii) the assignment is within the bounds that can be inferred from the values reported in *e* given the calibrations of the instruments warranted by *T*.

Relative to *T* the report *e* disconfirms *T* just in case from every assignment of values to parameters within the *T*-tolerance of *e* it is possible, with or without the help of premises drawn from *T*, to derive an inconsistency with *T*.

Explication of confirmation relative to *T* is rather more problematic. An obvious hunch here is the Popperian one that for *e* to confirm *T* the experiment whose outcome *e* reports must have been a 'potential falsifier' of *T*. A tempting way of spelling this out is to say that *e* provides *T*-confirmation of *T* just in case:

(i) it reports the outcome of measurements adequately performed (as judged from the standpoint of *T*);

(ii) it does not provide *T*-disconfirmation of *T*;

(iii) there exists an assignment of values to the parameters that figure in *e* from which, with or without the help of premises drawn from *T*, it is possible to derive an inconsistency with *T*.

This account has, however, an unfortunate consequence: it allows *T*-confirmation by reports of the outcomes of adequately performed measurements that could never have yielded a *T*-disconfirmation, simply because no combination of values of the relevant parameters that lies within the ranges of the measurement procedures is inconsistent with the theory.[3] To take an artificial example, suppose that *H* is the hypothesis: 'There do not exist objects with densities

---

[3] Cf. Glymour, *Theory and Evidence*, 115–16.

greater than 10^{16} gm/cc.' Consider reports of adequate measurements of volumes and weights of bodies by means, respectively, of displacement of water from a graduated cylinder and of a simple beam balance. The proposed account will, absurdly, make all such reports come out as confirmations of H. To avoid this sort of counter-example we define the T-range of an experimental report e as the set of assignments of values to the parameters which figure in it which lie within the ranges of the measurement procedures whose outcome it reports, where those ranges are judged from the standpoint of T. We then say that e provides T-confirmation of T just in case:

(i) it reports the outcomes of measurements adequately performed (as judged from the standpoint of T);

(ii) it does not provide T-disconfirmation of T;

(iii) there exists an assignment of values to the parameters of e within its T-range from which, with or without the help of premisses drawn from T, it is possible to derive an inconsistency with T.

The type of evidential equivalence of interest to us may now be specified. T_1 is evidentially equivalent to T_2, relative to a set of background theories T, a set of measurement procedures M, and a set of objects and systems K, just in case, for all experimental reports e of the outcomes of application of measurement procedures in M to objects and systems in K:

(i) e provides T-disconfirmation of T_1 if, and only if, e provides T-disconfirmation of T_2;

(ii) e provides T-confirmation of T_1 if, and only if, e provides T-confirmation of T_2.

We now possess the means to offer a measure of clarification of the informal account of reduction offered above. Let T be the set of theories held by protagonists of theory T; let M' be the measurement procedures available to protagonists of theory T'; and let K' be the range of objects and systems accessible to protagonists of T'. A first shot at an account of reduction is as follows:

R T' is reducible to T if, and only if, there is a theory T^* derivable from T (if necessary with the help of boundary conditions, bridge laws, auxiliary hypotheses, etc.), such that T^* is evidentially equivalent to T' given T, M', and K'.

In setting up this account certain difficulties have been glossed over. For example, serious and intractable problems of analysis are raised by cases in which a theory is impugned by an experimental report in deviant ways.[4] Further, it must be conceded that the postulation of a single consistent set of background theories held by protagonists of a given theory, a single set of measurement procedures available to them, and a single range of objects and systems accessible to them, involves gross simplifications. But perhaps the most glaring omission is the failure to discuss the ways in which background theory enters into the calibration of instruments and into the warranting of judgements about the adequacies of performances of measurement procedures. I touch on this topic again in Chapter VII, but even there the treatment is impressionistic.

R clearly covers cases of reducibility in which the reduced theory can be exhibited as a consequence of the reducing theory, the kind of case that inspired the 'classical' account of reducibility as a species of derivability and of which the reducibility of physical optics to classical electromagnetic theory provides a striking instance.[5] Individual phenomenological laws and small bodies of relatively low-level theory have often yielded to such strict reduction. But at the level of entire theories strict reduction is comparatively rare. In the majority of the paradigms of reduction—classical celestial mechanics to special relativistic celestial mechanics and the phenomenological thermodynamics of closed systems to statistical thermodynamics, for example—the reduced

---

[4] A host of ways can be thought up in which an experimental report may impugn a theory without in the sense defined here disconfirming it. Thus when a measurement procedure is inadequately performed or the instrument malfunctions the resultant experimental report may nevertheless impugn a theory, provided the bias introduced can be estimated. More ingeniously, cases in which an experimental report is triggered by post-hypnotic suggestion can be so contrived as to make an experimental report impugn a theory regardless of its content and even though no one can be said to have carried out a measurement. It is tempting to say of some of these impugnments that the experimental report does under some description disconfirm the theory, but not under the description 'experimental report'; of others it seems misleading under any description to say that the report disconfirms the theory, because its role in the disconfirmation is insufficiently central. Similar problems concerned with reliable indication of states of affairs brought about by 'deviant' causal chains are notorious in the theory of perception: see, e.g., C. Peacocke, *Holistic Explanation: Action, Space, Interpretation*, Oxford, 1979, ch. 2; and J. Heil, *Perception and Cognition*, Berkeley, 1983, ch. 6.

[5] K. F. Schaffner has suggested that this is not an exact derivation: 'Approaches to reduction', *Philosophy of Science*, 34 (1967), 137–47. But see R. M. Yoshida's rebuttal of this: *Reduction in the Physical Sciences*, Halifax, Nova Scotia, 1977, 32–5.

theory, far from being derivable from the reducing theory, is inconsistent with it. These paradigms are, however, covered by R.

Consider Max Born's assertion about the relation between classical and relativistic mechanics. 'Particular interest attaches to the limiting case in which the velocity v of the two [inertial] systems becomes very small in comparison with the velocity of light. We then arrive directly at the Galileo transformation.'[6] In what respect is v/c such that it can be neglected here? My suggestion is that it is negligible in precisely the sense that its difference from zero is undetectable by applying the apparatus available to protagonists of the classical theory to the systems accessible to them. As Born goes on to observe, 'Thus we understand how, on account of the small value that v/c has in most practical cases, Galilean and Newtonian mechanics satisfied all requirements for some centuries.'[7]

This is, I conjecture, the pattern common to all such approximative reductions. Counterfactual conditions are sought which differ negligibly, in the sense specified, from their actual counterparts in the reducing theory, but which when substituted for those counterparts transform a part of the reducing theory into the reduced theory. So the recipe for approximative reduction of T' to T is as follows. Attempt to find a subtheory of T, T^*, that can itself be decomposed into a theory or theory-schema T^{**} and a set of conditions C in such a way that for some alternative set of conditions C':

(i) T^{**} & C is evidentially equivalent to T^{**} & C' relative to the background theories held by protagonists of T, the measurement procedures available to protagonists of T', and the objects and systems accessible to protagonists of T';

(ii) T^{**} & $C' = T'$ [8]

If the recipe works, T' is clearly reducible to T according to

    [6] *Einstein's Theory of Relativity*, rev. edn., New York, 1962, p. 237.

    [7] Ibid., p. 238.

    [8] In case $T^* = T$ our account becomes quite close to Yoshida's account of theoretical transformation: *Reduction in the Physical Sciences*, 74–6. The main difference concerns the extent to which the conditions C' may conflict with the reducing theory T: Yoshida requires that the counterfactual conditions be incompatible only with 'non-essential' statements of T. Our account has affinities also with H. R. Post's classic account of intertheoretic reduction: 'Correspondence, invariance and heuristics: in praise of conservative induction', *Studies in History and Philosophy of Science*, 2 (1971), 213–55.

condition R set out above. So our account covers approximative reductions.

The capacity of R to capture the paradigms of reduction provides a measure of confirmation for it as an explication of reduction, as well as providing a modicum of encouragement for the view that reducibility has been prevalent in the history of science. But on the latter score it may well be objected that the paradigm reductions, both strict and approximative, are didactic myths—when we look at past theories warts and all, rather than at the retrospectively rationalized and refurbished versions that populate textbooks, such tidy reductions are rarely to be found. The objection is not damaging to our case. Prevalence of reducibility of substantial parts of past theories suffices for our purposes, and the paradigm textbook cases surely have at least this basis in the real as opposed to the didactic history of science.

The textbook paradigms of reduction are specialized in another respect as well, as they involve relatively simple and uniform bridge-laws relating terms of the reduced theory to terms of the reducing theory. Once it is allowed that the bridge-laws that link past theories to present ones may be both complex and context sensitive, the case for the prevalence of reduction is greatly strengthened. Consider, for example, the relations between classical transmission genetics and molecular biology.[9] If we insist that the classical term 'gene' be rendered uniformly and simply into the language of molecular biology, then not even a partial reduction will be forthcoming. But suppose we admit complex and contextually determined renderings of classical terms, 'gene', for example, being translated in one way when it describes a unit of recombination, in another when it describes a unit of mutation, and so on. Then it becomes arguable that classical genetics is at least partially reducible (via fine-structure genetics) to molecular biology. Such cases can be multiplied. Indeed, even phlogiston theory and caloric theory, the exemplars of theories fated to be replaced rather than reduced, become strong candidates for having been partially reduced by their successors once complex and non-uniform inter-

---

[9] On the relations between transmission genetics and molecular biology see K. F. Schaffner, 'The Watson–Crick model and reductionism', *British Journal for the Philosophy of Science*, 20 (1969), 325–48; P. Kitcher, 'Genes', *British Journal for the Philosophy of Science*, 33 (1982), 337–59; and R. Falk, 'What is a gene?', *Studies in History and Philosophy of Science*, 17 (1986).

theoretic explications are allowed.[10]

Does R specify a sufficient condition for reducibility? This seems doubtful on several scores. First, note that both strict and approximative reductions entail significantly more than the required sort of evidential equivalence between the reduced theory T' and a part T^* of the reducing theory T. In each case it is by virtue of common theoretical content—the theory T' itself in the case of strict reduction and the theory or theory-schema T^{**} in the case of approximative reduction—that the evidential equivalence holds. Secondly, the historical cases of reduction with which we are concerned are all cases in which the reducing theory is logically stronger than the common ground between the two theories. These two conditions together ensure that from the standpoint of the reducing theory the reduction involves an accumulation of theoretical truth. Further conditions that are satisfied by all the examples that concern us have to do with the empirical contents of the reduced and reducing theories. There is, first, the condition that the reduced theory be empirically non-vacuous from the standpoint of the reducing theory, that is, that it be T-confirmable by means available to its protagonists. A second condition is that the reducing theory have some edge on the reduced theory in the matter of confirmation— that is, that there be experimental outcomes that T-confirm it, but not the reduced theory.

It is a moot point whether these, and perhaps other triviality-evading and monster-barring conditions, should be added to R to ensure its sufficiency. Instead of pursuing this analytical point I shall call intertheoretic relations that satisfy the condition of partial empirical equivalence set out in R together with all four of the above conditions 'non-trivial reductions'. Non-trivial reductions have, I claim, been prevalent in the history of science.

Let us now turn from the question of prevalence of non-trivial reductions to the question of the implications of non-trivial reducibility. Scientists expend very considerable effort in attempts to

[10] N. Koertge, 'A Study of Relations between Scientific Theories: a Test of the General Correspondence Principle', unpublished Ph.D. thesis, London, 1969, provides a historically detailed defence of the claim that many explanatorily effective theories generally taken to have been replaced were in fact partially reduced by their successors. On the partial reducibility of Stahlian phlogiston theory see Koertge, ibid., 131–234, and P. Kitcher, 'Theories, theorists and theoretical change', *The Philosophical Review*, 87 (1978), 119–47. On the partial reducibility of caloric theory see Yoshida, *Reduction in the Physical Sciences*, 68–70.

exhibit past theories as reducible to their own. Why? The philosophical literature contains a wide diversity of suggestions about the functions of reduction that might serve to explain this interest: unification of theories, ontological simplification, explanation of the reduced theory, explanation of the extent to which the reduced theory succeeded, acquisition by the reducing theory of evidence that supported the reduced theory.[11]

Of these the last is partly vindicated by our account of reduction. If T' is reducible to T, then T'-confirmatory evidence available to protagonists of T' also T-confirms a subtheory T^* of T; and likewise for T-disconfirmation. There can, of course, be no general guarantee that evidence that T-confirms T^* will not T-disconfirm T as a whole: for one and the same experimental report may be relevant to two (or more) subtheories of a theory, confirming one while disconfirming another. With this proviso, reduction has all the advantages of theft over honest toil in the business of confirmation. Suppose, as is commonly the case, that a past theory is known to have been confirmed by a wide range of observations and experiments. To secure that confirmation for some theory of his own the scientist appears at first sight to have just two options: *either*, when he has access to past experimental reports he may check case by case whether they confirm his theory; *or*, when he has no such records (or has insufficient information about the adequacy of the performances whose outcomes they report to enable him to tell whether or not they confirm his theory), he may repeat the experiments one by one. Not so! There is a far easier way. If the past theory can be reduced to his own, whatever confirmation of it was available to its protagonists accrues to a subtheory of his own. In practice, despite the above proviso, that generally means that the confirmation accrues to his theory as a whole.[12] This will, for example, always happen when the subject-matter of the subtheory of the reducing

---

[11] For a survey of the diverse functions that have been attributed to theoretical reduction see W. C. Wimsatt, 'Reduction and reductionism', in P. D. Asquith and H. E. Kyburg, *Current Research in Philosophy of Science*, E. Lansing, Michigan, 1979, 352–77. Views on the functions of reduction related in certain respects to those developed here are expressed by Yoshida, *Reduction in the Physical Sciences*; M. Friedman, 'Theoretical explanation', in R. Healey, ed., *Reduction, Time and Reality: Studies in the Philosophy of the Natural Sciences*, Cambridge, 1981, 1–16; and P. M. Churchland, *Scientific Realism and the Plasticity of Mind*, Cambridge, 1979, ch. 11.

[12] Yoshida, *Reduction in the Physical Sciences*, p. 72, cites a couple of examples of explicit recognition of this principle in physics textbooks.

theory that is evidentially equivalent to the reduced theory is entirely distinct from the subject-matters of other parts of the theory. Even when the subject-matters of different parts of the reducing theory overlap, there will often be no question of confirmatory evidence from one part providing disconfirmation for other parts, because the parameters that are relevant to the different parts may be very different: freely falling harmonic oscillators are in the domains of two very different applications of classical dynamics, but it does not follow that experiments designed to test the laws of free fall can have outcomes relevant to the dynamics of harmonic oscillators. Finally, even when the evidential domain of the part of the reducing theory that is evidentially equivalent to the reduced theory does overlap with the evidential domains of other parts of the reducing theory, the supposition that confirmatory evidence carried over from the reduced theory might 'accidentally' disconfirm some distinct part of the reducing theory may be very far fetched. In principle, for example, confirmatory evidence for transmission genetics that carried over to the biochemistry of ribonucleic acid via the partial reduction of transmission genetics to molecular biology might accidentally disconfirm fundamental laws of chemistry (concerning, say, valency or the nature of the hydrogen bond). But, though on the cards, it is most unlikely that the ratio of red to white-eyed fruit flies in some sample should in fact disconfirm fundamental laws of chemistry, given the massive confirmation of those laws by far more direct means and the lack of any reason whatsoever for thinking their application to ribonucleic acids to be problematic.

The securing of confirmation for present theories from the domains of evidence for past theories does not provide the only motive for interest in reduction. Consider the 'realist' thesis that theories that are highly confirmed are probably true. This assumption underlies, amongst other heuristic principles, the principle of conservatism according to which one should seek to preserve the well-confirmed parts of existing theories when constructing new theories. The connection between confirmation and truth would, however, be undermined were the history of science to reveal many past theories that are by our lights both highly confirmed and false. If confirmation is indicative of truth, we should expect the history of science to show past theories that are well confirmed from the standpoint of our theories to have substantial components that are true from the standpoint of our theories. This may be regarded as a weak form of the so-called 'correspondence principle'.[13] It is confirmed by the prevalence of non-trivial reducibility of past theories to current theories, for in each case the reduced theory is well confirmed over a particular domain of evidence (the evidence available to its protagonists), provided that the reducing theory is well confirmed by that evidence. If the reduction is a strict one the reduced theory is true from the standpoint of the reducing theory. If the reduction is approximative, then the reduced theory will have a substantial component true from the standpoint of the reducing theory. So in both sorts of reduction to current theories the link between confirmation and truth is vindicated.

Our immediate concern with reduction is not, however, with its scientific role in the confirmation of theories or with its methodological role in the vindication of the principle of conservatism. Rather, our appeal to the prevalence of reduction is intended to secure a major part of the historical evidence on which the thesis of scientific absolutism rests. If non-trivial reducibility of past theories to current ones is widespread, then, as has already been noted, there has been widespread accumulation of what are, from the standpoint of current theories, general truths. Further, in approximative reductions, the commonest type of reduction, transcendence of error is generally seen, from the standpoint of the reducing theory, to have occurred. For in approximative reductions, whilst the reduced theory is partially false from the standpoint of the reducing theory, the discrepancies between the two theories are such that they cannot be detected by any experimental or observational set-up available to protagonists of the reduced theory. Typically the extra confirmation available to the reducing theory comes in part from observations or experiments that do discriminate the two theories. So protagonists of the reducing theory may explain the shortcomings of the reduced theory in terms of the liability of its protagonists to a systematic source of error, namely the limited range of the data available to them (often itself, in turn, to be explained in terms of the limited discriminatory powers of their instruments). A similar type of explanation will often be

[13] Post, 'Correspondence, invariance and heuristics', and N. Koertge, 'Theory change in science', in G. Pearce and P. Maynard, eds., *Conceptual Change*, Dordrecht, 1973, 167–98, defend slightly stronger versions of the correspondence principle. W. Krajewski, *The Correspondence Principle and the Growth of Science*, Dordrecht, 1977, maintains a much stronger version.

available in cases of partial reduction. Here, provided the reducing theory is well confirmed by evidence of types not available to protagonists of the reduced theory, it will often be open to protagonists of the reducing theory to explain the shortcomings of unreduced parts of the partially reduced theory in terms of limitations on the evidence available to protagonists of that theory. Thus we see that the prevalence of reducibility and partial reducibility of past theories to our own theories, entailing as it does both widespread resolution of general questions and widespread transcendence of error, underwrites an important part of the historical evidence needed for the defence of scientific absolutism.

Only the third and boldest of the claims made at the beginning of the chapter remains to be argued for. This is the claim that when a sound case can be made for reduction of a past theory to a current theory, that case cannot be undermined on the scores of incommensurability of theories or indeterminacy of intertheoretic interpretation. As a first step in the exploration of the connections between reduction and interpretation, let us relativize all claims about the relations between theories to intertheoretic interpretation schemes. In what follows the theory that is reduced, or is a candidate for reduction, under an interpretation scheme will be called 'the target theory', the theory that reduces it, or aspires to do so, being designated 'the base theory'.

Reducibility relative to an arbitrary intertheoretic interpretation scheme is not an interesting relation. To contrive trivial instances one has merely to set up interpretation schemes under which the measurement procedures employed by protagonists of the target theory are not, from the standpoint of the base theory and the background theories associated with it, valid procedures for measuring the parameters with which protagonists of the target theory are interpreted as associating them. Such an interpretation scheme, by depriving the target theory of its empirical content, makes reduction a trivial matter.

To avoid such trivialization it is tempting to confine our attention to interpretation schemes which so explicate parameter terms of the target theory as to allow us, on the whole, to construe protagonists of that theory as performers of valid measurement procedures. This condition on interpretation schemes is, however, too crude. Suppose an interpretation scheme construes protagonists of a target theory as users of invalid measurement procedures for certain parameters, whilst at the same time so interpreting other beliefs of theirs as to render their use of the invalid procedures explicable (in terms, for example, of their having a partial or incorrect understanding of the workings of the instruments involved). Here the attribution of use of invalid measurement procedures that the interpretation scheme entails in no way counts against it. The required condition on interpretation schemes is rather that they should not entail attribution of inexplicable use of invalid measurement procedures to protagonists of the target theory. I shall call interpretation schemes that satisfy this condition 'empirically adequate'.

an empirically adequate interpretation scheme *I*, then from the standpoint of an interpreter who holds *T*, *I* is a good interpretation scheme.

To start with we note that such an interpretation scheme has, for the protagonist of *T*, a notable virtue simply on account of its empirical adequacy, quite apart from whatever virtues may be entailed by its reduction-inducing powers. It is surely a virtue in an interpretation scheme that it should as far as possible allow the interpreter to credit the subjects whose behaviour is under scrutiny with mastery of their own language. That requires, amongst a great many other things, that under the interpretation scheme they be seen to manifest a grasp of the senses of their predicates. And that, in turn, requires that under the interpretation scheme attribution of inexplicable misapplication of those predicates should, other things being equal, be minimized. In the case of predicates which figure in experimental reports, to meet this requirement is precisely to satisfy the empirical adequacy condition.

Now let us consider some of the ways in which the standing of an empirically adequate interpretation scheme may be further enhanced should it induce a non-trivial reduction of the target theory to a theory held by the interpreter. A second virtue in an interpretation scheme is that it should, by and large, construe the subjects of interpretation as reasonable in their beliefs. If *T'* is reducible to *T* under an empirically adequate interpretation scheme *I*, then from the standpoint of *T* it can be inferred that, save under special circumstances, the outcomes of observations and experiments carried out by protagonists of *T'* would have appeared to them to confirm *T'*. The exceptional circumstances include various sorts of observational and inferential errors on the part of protagonists of T'. They also include certain cases in which experimental set-ups available to protagonists of T' yield results that T-disconfirm the part of the base theory T that is empirically equivalent to the target theory T'—that is, they include certain experimental outcomes that the interpreter is bound to regard as genuinely anomalous. So I fares well with regard to at least one sort of reasonableness of belief, namely reasonableness with regard to empirical confirmation and disconfirmation of general beliefs. Reasonableness with regard to confirmation and disconfirmation of general beliefs may be regarded as a special case of a more general category of reasonable-ness, that of not knowingly entertaining inconsistent beliefs—the inconsistencies to be avoided here being between singular beliefs based on the outcomes of experiments and the general beliefs which they may instantiate or counter-instantiate. An interpretation scheme which induces a non-trivial reduction to a theory held by the interpreter attributes this category of reasonableness to the subjects of interpretation in another way as well. For it ensures that the entire target theory (in the case of a strict reduction) or a substantial part of it (in the case of an approximative reduction) is consistent provided only that the reducing theory is consistent. Finally, it should be added that empirically adequate interpretation schemes which induce non-trivial reductions often achieve distinction in respect of a third virtue of interpretation, that of minimizing attribution of inexplicably false beliefs. The condition is obviously satisfied for exact reductions, in which the reduced theory is true from the standpoint of the reducing theory; and, as we have already seen, both approximative and partial reductions typically give rise to explanations of the past acceptance of partially false theories in terms of the limited availability of evidence to their holders.

Now, let us consider the question of the adequacy of an interpret-ation scheme for the specific purpose of explicating a particular target theory and the body of observational and experimental practice associated with it. I suggest that in this context possession of the virtues detailed above suffices to certify it as an adequate interpretation scheme. So we have the following:

A If T' is non-trivially reducible to T under an empirically adequate interpretation scheme I, then, from the standpoint of T, I is an adequate interpretation scheme for the purpose of expli-cating T'.

I shall call this 'the adequacy principle'. Setting aside for the moment the pressing question of the legitimacy of relativization of interpretation schemes to interpretive projects, we note that the adequacy principle suffices to defeat the claim that incommensurability of theories invalidates all reducibility claims.

In our attempt to head off the threat to reducibility claims posed by indeterminacy of intertheoretic interpretation we cannot, I suspect, hope to show that when T' is non-trivially reducible to T under an empirically adequate interpretation scheme I, I is from the standpoint of T a uniquely optimal interpretation scheme for the purpose of explicating T'. For this is gainsaid if it is ever possible for there to be more than one empirically adequate interpretation scheme that induces a given reduction. Field and Sklar have offered convincing examples of variant interpretation schemes under which a given intertheoretic reduction holds.[14]

A considerably weaker thesis, still sufficient to block the threat to reducibility claims for indeterminacy of interpretation, is as follows. If T' is non-trivially reducible to T under an empirically adequate interpretation scheme I, then I is, from the standpoint of T, a better interpretation scheme for the purpose of explicating T' than is any scheme under which T' is not non-trivially reducible to T. This would provide an elegant complement to A; but it is, I fear, still too strong. Consider empirically adequate interpretation schemes I, I', where T' is non-trivially reducible to T under I, and T' is partially, though almost completely, non-trivially reducible to T under I'. Surely under these circumstances the preferability of I is not guaranteed. Suppose, for example, I were far less simple than I'. A slightly weaker claim does, however, seem warranted:

O   If T' is non-trivially reducible to T under an empirically adequate interpretation scheme I, then, from the standpoint of T, I is better than any interpretation scheme under which T' is not at least partially non-trivially reducible to T.

This I shall call 'the optimality principle'.
The optimality principle suffices, by the skin of its teeth, to

---

[14] H. Field, 'Theory change and indeterminacy of reference', *The Journal of Philosophy*, 60 (1972), 462–81; L. Sklar, 'Thermodynamics, statistical mechanics and the complexity of reductions', in R. S. Cohen *et al.*, eds., *Boston Studies in the Philosophy of Science*, vol. 32, Dordrecht, 1976, 15–52. Field's claim has been challenged by Yoshida, *Reduction in the Physical Sciences*, Appendix, and J. Earman, 'Against indeterminacy', *The Journal of Philosophy*, 74 (1977), 535–8.

counter the threat to reducibility claims that is posed by the thesis of indeterminacy of intertheoretic interpretation. To see this, equate non-trivial reducibility with non-trivial reducibility under every optimal interpretation scheme. From O it follows that if T' is non-trivially reducible to T under an interpretation scheme optimal from the standpoint of T for the explication of T', it is at least partially non-trivially reducible to T under every interpretation scheme optimal from the standpoint of T for the explication of T'.

If it is legitimate to relativize questions of adequacy of interpretation scheme to such interpretive projects as explication of a particular past theory, then we have achieved our aim. We have shown well-founded reducibility claims to be exempt from the threats posed by incommensurability and indeterminacy of intertheoretic interpretation. There is, however, a cogent objection to this type of relativization.

Interpretation is generally taken to involve a particular type of holism, holism in respect of the evidence. An interpretation scheme cannot, so the holistic thesis has it, be broken down into segments, each segment being answerable to evidence drawn from some particular domain of the behaviour of the subjects of interpretation. Rather, each component of an interpretation scheme is potentially answerable to evidence from every domain of the behaviour of the subjects of interpretation. To see such diffusion of answerability in action suppose that we—holders of theory T—have arrived at an interpretation scheme I solely on the basis of behaviour by protagonists of theory T' that we construe (under that interpretation scheme) as having to do with their holding of T': performance of experiments to test T', discussion of the metaphysical foundations of T', utterance of hypotheses of T', axiomatization of T', etc. Let us suppose too that T' is non-trivially reducible to T under I and that I is, on the evidence considered, empirically adequate as well. The holistic thesis may be illustrated in two ways by considering outcomes of the attempt to extend I to cover other theories held by the protagonists of T'. First, it may turn out in the light of evidence relating to their performance of experiments in connection with theories that I is not, after all, empirically adequate. Secondly, it may turn out that all attempts to extend I to the other theories fare very badly by the various criteria for explication of theories, making them appear complex, inconsistent, and ill-confirmed by the evidence available to their protagonists, etc. It may happily be conceded that in the first case *I* is discredited. If further evidence shows an interpretation scheme not to be empirically adequate, then it is hard to see how it can serve any legitimate interpretive purpose. In the second example, however, we cannot, on pain of having to abandon A and O, concede that *I* is discredited.

As a first step in countering this apparently fatal objection, let us note a difference between the ways in which an initially promising interpretation scheme is undermined in these examples. In the first instance, the one in which the empirical adequacy of the scheme is refuted, no change in interpretive project is involved—rather, an interpretation scheme is shown to be inadequate for all purposes including its originally intended purpose, that of explicating a particular past theory. In the second instance, however, the situation is, rather, that an interpretation scheme adequate for one interpretive purpose is shown to be inadequate for others.

Underlying the doctrine of holism of interpretation in respect of the evidence is a certain hermeneutic ideal. The proper starting-point of interpretation is supposed to be as full as possible a register of 'raw' information about the behaviour of the subjects of interpretation—their bodily movements and the sounds they emit—and of the circumstances under which such activity is manifested. The proper end-product is envisaged as a single total interpretation scheme within which all aspects of the subjects' behaviour are so regimented as to reveal their rationality to the highest attainable degree. I shall call this 'the ideal of radical interpretation'.[15] Exponents of the ideal of radical interpretation have offered diverse accounts of what constitutes rationality on the part of subjects of interpretation. But despite varied conceptions of rationality, those who subscribe to this ideal share a view of the interpreter's activity as one of rationalization of the totality of the subjects' behaviour in the light of the totality of their perceptions, standing beliefs, desires, etc. Holism of interpretation in respect of the evidence is inevitable given such an ideal.

Actual interpretive projects differ from the project of radical interpretation in obvious respects: we never start with absolutely raw behavioural data, unsullied by all interpretive preconceptions; and life is too short for us to hope to achieve such all-embracing

[15] The most complete and explicit articulation of this ideal that I know is by D. Lewis, 'Radical interpretation', *Synthese*, 23 (1974), 331–44; reprinted with appendices in *Philosophical Papers*, vol. 1, Oxford, 1983, 108–21.

interpretation schemes. But in these respects the idealization is surely legitimate. There is, however, a much more basic divergence between interpretive practice and this interpretive ideal. Real-life interpretive projects are inevitably piecemeal, setting out to illuminate particular aspects of the subjects' activities, beliefs, and mores—their political organization, their religious practices, their domestic behaviour and kinship structure, their alchemy, their medical lore, etc. The amalgamation of a multiplicity of projects for the interpretation of given subjects into a single all-encompassing project is not, I suggest, a legitimate idealization. To see why, let us consider briefly the connection between our interpretive projects and the various projects that may be attributed to subjects of interpretation.

It is scarcely controversial to claim that to achieve understanding of others we must attempt to find meanings for their actions in terms of the projects in which they are engaged. Radical interpretation would constitute a legitimate ideal in the quest for understanding of subjects who could legitimately be construed as 'one-dimensional persons' engaged in a single vast project. Suppose, however, that we envisage the subjects of interpretation as being participants in many projects, showing substantial measures of coherence in behaviour within the bounds of each project, but subject in their beliefs, desires, and actions to no single overarching scheme of rationality. The ideal of interpretation that fits this model is that of a multiplicity of interpretive projects, each seeking to optimize the rationality of the subjects of interpretation within the bounds set by one of their projects.

Defence of 'many-dimensional man' is far beyond the scope of this work. However, a line of thought conducive to such a model deserves mention. Subjects of interpretation customarily interpret their own activities as pursuit of a multiplicity of independent projects rather than as furtherances of a single master-project. Whilst there are cogent grounds for denying exclusive privilege to subjects' self-interpretations, it appears a sound principle not to attribute to subjects inexplicable misconstruals of their own activities. So in the absence of a plausible explanation for a general tendency among subjects of interpretation to fail to apprehend the master-projects which inform their actions, we have a prima facie case for many-dimensional man. To strengthen the case for many dimensional man it is, I suspect, necessary to become more deeply involved in philosophical anthropology and to reflect on the multiplicities of social roles persons occupy and the diversity of the discursive practices in which they partake.[16]

To convert this bare sketch of a 'piecemeal' ideal of interpretation into a fully fledged theory of interpretation would be a major undertaking indeed. In particular, it would require the construction and defence of an account of the ways in which the totality of activities of subjects of interpretation may be carved up into more or less autonomous projects. For present purposes, however, it suffices to note that the construction, defence, and application of a theory in some domain of scientific inquiry is a paradigm of a semi-autonomous project.

In the context of the many-dimensional model of man and the associated piecemeal ideal of interpretation the impact of the holistic objection to A and O, the principles of adequacy and optimality of interpretation introduced earlier, is diminished. The holistic objection remains effective when the theories with whose reduction we are concerned are isolated hypotheses or subtheories. But if A and O are qualified to apply only to full-scale theories that can reasonably be taken as the foci of distinct cognitive projects of the subjects of interpretation, the force of the objection is dispelled. I conclude that our case for the adequacy of interpretation schemes that induce non-trivial reductions holds good in the face of holistic considerations.

We have completed the main business of this chapter: the defence of a major part of the historical evidence for scientific absolutism against the threats posed by intertheoretic incommensurability and indeterminacy of intertheoretic interpretation. There are, however, a number of important points arising out of the foregoing discussion that deserve mention before we turn away from hermeneutic matters.

All the various virtues of empirically adequate reduction-inducing interpretation schemes that we have reviewed may be considered as instances of a single super-virtue, the virtue of minimizing attribution of inexplicable error that is sometimes called

[16] The multiplicity of independent projects by which an agent may be possessed is wonderfully portrayed in Robert Musil's *The Man without Qualities* [1930], English trans. by E. Wilkins and E. Kaiser, London, 1953. More sober materials for a philosophical defence of many-dimensional man are to be found in Clifford Geertz's *The Interpretation of Cultures*, New York, 1973, and *Local Knowledge*, New York, 1983, and in the essays in J. Elster, ed., *The Multiple Self*, Cambridge, 1986.

'humanity of interpretation'.[17] Thus the first virtue listed concerned the minimization of attribution of the inexplicable misapplication of predicates; the second concerned the minimization of attribution of the inexplicable holding of inconsistent beliefs; and the third concerned the minimization of attribution of the inexplicable holding of false general beliefs. When past or alien theories are dominated by our theories, there is, from the standpoint of our theories, an explanation of the existence of false components in the other theories in terms of error or limitation in the procedures that gave rise to them. The question naturally arises whether by appeal to the principle of humanity we can defend domination claims as well as reduction claims from the threats posed by incommensurability and by indeterminacy of interpretation, thus securing yet more of the historical evidence appealed to in our defence of scientific absolutism. My hunch is that domination claims can indeed be defended in this way.

The principle of humanity of interpretation has further important consequences connected with the question of the extent to which our beliefs may be false. Satisfaction of the principle by an interpretation scheme is compatible with, and may indeed require, attribution of falsity to the beliefs of others on a substantial scale. This is evident when an interpretation scheme satisfies the principle of humanity by inducing an approximative reduction of some past theory to a theory of our own. From the standpoint of the reducing theory such an interpretation scheme is typically seen as rendering many of the principles and laws of the reduced theory into falsehoods. When we turn to other modes of dominance of one theory by another it is easy to envisage situations in which satisfaction of the principle of humanity would require us to attribute falsehood on a much larger scale: one has only to cook up hypothetical cases in which we systematically explain the theoretical beliefs of others in terms of wholesale misinformation about the relevant phenomena occasioned, for example, by their erroneous beliefs about the functioning of measurement instruments or by their having been

---

[17] The term comes from R. E. Grandy, 'Reference, meaning, and belief', *The Journal of Philosophy*, 70 (1973), 439–52. However, Grandy's principle 'that the imputed pattern of relations among beliefs, desires and the world be as similar to our own as possible' is much more general. For an informative discussion of the principle (and references to some of the now substantial literature on it) see S. Lukes, 'Relativism in its place', in M. Hollis and S. Lukes, eds., *Rationality and Relativism*, Cambridge, 1982, 261–305, pp. 262–9.

misled by a well-orchestrated programme of dissemination of fraudulent data.

Is there a limit to the extent of attribution of false beliefs that may be licensed by the principle of humanity of interpretation? When satisfaction of the principle ensues from approximative reduction the answer is clearly affirmative. In an approximative reduction, whilst some or all of the experimental laws of the reduced theory are false from the standpoint of the reducing theory, a substantial body of beliefs about the mutual dependences of values of measurable parameters is common to the two theories. In explaining why protagonists of the reduced theory held false beliefs this body of beliefs about measurable parameters plays an indispensable part. For it is by virtue of their holding of those beliefs that it can be seen why the entire reduced theory seemed to its protagonists to be confirmed. A similar body of beliefs true from the explainer's standpoint is presupposed in other cases of satisfaction of the principle of humanity through extensive attribution of false beliefs. Thus any explanation of the holding of false beliefs in terms of a misunderstanding of the workings of measurement instruments is bound to involve attribution of some true beliefs about the workings of the instruments—on pain of incoherence in interpreting their use as the carrying out of measurements—as well as true beliefs about the readings given by the instruments on particular occasions; and explanation of wholesale falsity in belief occasioned by acceptance of fraudulent data involves attribution of true beliefs about what the misinformants said the data were and about the ways in which the false data relate to certain theories. Though satisfaction of the principle of humanity may require the attribution of extensive falsehood in belief to the subjects of interpretation, it requires also the attribution of a core of true beliefs.[18]

Earlier it was suggested that an account of truth would be deeply

---

[18] Notoriously, much stronger conclusions have sometimes been drawn from this kind of 'bridgehead' argument. Davidson, for example, concludes that 'if we want to understand others, we must count them right in most matters', 'On the very idea of a conceptual scheme', *Proceedings and Addresses of the American Philosophical Association*, 47 (1973–4), 5–20, p. 19; and M. Hollis concludes that the sharing of 'our concepts of truth, coherence and rational interdependence of beliefs' is a necessary condition of interpretability, 'The limits of irrationality', *Archives Européenes de Sociologie*, 7 (1967), 265–71. Cogent objections to the more ambitious uses of the 'bridgehead' strategy are to be found in W. Newton-Smith, 'Relativism and the possibility of interpretation', in Hollis and Lukes, eds., *Rationality and Relativism*, 106–22.

suspect were it incompatible with the epistemic elusiveness of truth, the possibility that a very substantial part of our current beliefs may be false. We are now in a position to substantiate the claim that our pragmatic account of truth meets this condition. On that account, the possibility that a substantial part of our beliefs might be false is equivalent to the possibility that they might be false from the standpoint of an absolute inquiry series. This, in turn, is a coherent supposition only if it can coherently be supposed that there could be interpreters (our future selves, for example) who found that our theories came out substantially false under an adequate interpretation scheme. If, as has been argued, interpretation schemes that induce approximative reductions (and perhaps other forms of domination of one theory by another) are on occasion both adequate and such as to attribute extensive falsity of belief, then this is a coherent supposition. However, the extreme form of the epistemic elusiveness thesis—that which concedes the possibility that all our beliefs might be false—is at odds with the claim that satisfaction of the principle of humanity is a necessary condition for adequate interpretation. For satisfaction of the principle of humanity of interpretation requires attribution of truth to at least some of the beliefs of the subjects of interpretation. So it is incoherent to suppose that there could be interpreters who found that all our beliefs came out false under an adequate interpretation scheme. On our pragmatic account of truth it follows immediately that it is incoherent to suppose that all our beliefs might be false.

The incompatibility of adequate interpretation with the attribution of wholesale falsity to the beliefs of the subjects of interpretation has a further consequence of considerable import for the defence of scientific absolutism. It precludes the possibility that we might one day, whether through an encounter with alien beings or through bifurcation of our science, find ourselves confronted with a total conflict of belief-systems. This is important because, for reasons touched on in the last chapter and to be elaborated in the next, it is only against a background of shared belief that we can hope to achieve reliable resolutions of theoretical conflict.

VI

Underdetermination of Theory

UNDERDETERMINATION of theory by empirical evidence—the existence of inconsistent theories the issue between which is irresoluble by any possible body of empirical evidence—threatens every one of the main claims about the capacities of human inquiry on which we have rested our defence of scientific absolutism. Directly it threatens the claim that human inquiry indefinitely prolonged under favourable circumstances has an unlimited capacity to resolve general scientific questions. Indirectly it threatens both the claim that such inquiry has an unlimited capacity to overcome sources of systematic error and the claim that it would prove resilient in the face of whatever alien inquiries may one day be encountered.

It is notoriously hard to find a formulation of the underdetermination thesis that is both coherent and such as to preserve the initial impact of the idea that inconsistent theories may be indiscernible 'come what may' in the way of outcomes of observation and experiment. In seeking such a formulation the sense of 'possible evidence' demands clarification, and the conditions under which a body of empirical evidence reliably resolves the issue between rival theories need spelling out. Further, and this is a requirement that seems especially hard to meet, the notion of empirical evidence needs to be articulated in a way that makes no illegitimate appeal to a sharp and theoretical context-free distinction between theory and observation.

'Possible evidence' admits a wide range of interpretations. At a pinch it may be so construed as to cover only evidence that will in due course have been gathered. At a stretch it may be taken to include not only evidence which could as a matter of physical possibility be gathered by suitably placed observers, but also evidence that is merely logically possible (perhaps to be construed as evidence available to observers suitably placed in other possible worlds). The narrow construal threatens to turn radical underdetermination of theory by data into a platitude; the broad construal threatens it with obvious falsity. Our concern is with a reading of intermediate breadth, according to which 'possible evidence' only embraces evidence that could, as a matter of physical possibility, be obtained by us humans.

The question of the conditions for resolution of theoretical conflict is readily answered by strict falsificationists who hold refutation of one of a pair of rival theories to be necessary for resolution of conflict. An underdetermination thesis appropriate to this falsificationist view is as follows. There exist empirically non-vacuous inconsistent theories T, T' such that, for all bodies of possible evidence E, E is compatible with both T and T'. This I shall call 'the weak underdetermination thesis', WU for short. Suppose instead that it is allowed that evidence compatible with rival theories may nevertheless support the rivals to different degrees, and hence in certain cases allow reliable resolution of conflict without falsification of either theory. A variety of underdetermination theses appropriate to this 'inductivist' view may be formulated.[1] One such is as follows. There exist empirically non-vacuous inconsistent theories T, T' such that, for all bodies of possible evidence E, E supports T and T' equally well, and supports no theory T'' better. I shall call this 'the strong underdetermination thesis', SU for short.

The difficulty in specifying a theoretical context-free notion of evidence is, I think, fatal to any attempt to spell out underdetermination theses by elaboration of conditions like those already set out. In the last chapter we touched on some of the ways in which the notions of evidence and evidential support are dependent on background theories; and well-known arguments show such dependence to be in principle ineliminable. It follows that underdetermination theses that quantify without qualification over bodies of evidence are incoherent. Any rejoicing by the defender of scientific absolutism at this dissolution of standard types of underdetermination theses would, however, be premature. For the threat re-emerges when we consider certain theses about the fortunes of human inquiry that are closely analogous to the weak and strong underdetermination theses set out above, but which allow for the dependence on theoretical context of the notions of evidence and evidential support.

---

[1] The labelling of this position 'inductivist' I derive from P. Horwich, 'How to choose between empirically indistinguishable theories', *The Journal of Philosophy*, 79 (1982), 61–77, p. 62.

As a first step towards the formulation of 'pragmatic' under-determination theses let us consider in the most schematic of terms the situation of a community of inquirers C faced with a conflict of theories T, T', against the background of a set of theories T that are not in dispute. Indicating the dependence of evidence on back-ground theory by appropriate prefixing, we say that the issue between T and T' is *strongly resolved* in C at time t just in case one or both of T, T' is inconsistent with the conjunction of T with the T-evidence possessed at t by C. Strong resolution is obviously not irreversible, since a change in background theory may affect either the domain of evidence or the impact of evidence on the conflicting theories. Consider now an indefinitely prolonged inquiry. We say that a conflict between theories T and T' is permanently strongly resolved just in case at some stage there occurs a strong resolution that is not overturned at any subsequent stage.

We may now formulate a pragmatic version of the weak under-determination thesis.

> PWU An indefinitely prolonged human inquiry would encounter theoretical conflicts for which it was unable to achieve permanent strong resolutions.

A pragmatic strong underdetermination thesis is not so readily articulated, for there are serious problems about the ways in which evidential support depends upon background theories. For the moment let us simply acknowledge the dependence. We then say that the issue between rival theories T, T' is *weakly resolved* in community C at time t just in case *either* one of T, T' is better T-supported by the T-evidence available to members of C at time t, *or* there is some third theory T'' entertained by members of C that is better T-supported by that T-evidence than is either T or T'. Weak resolutions, like strong resolutions, may be undone by a change in background theory. In addition they may be overthrown even without a change in background theory, either as a result of the discovery of new evidence or as a result of the construction of new theories in the same domain of inquiry.

We may now formulate a pragmatic strong underdetermination thesis.

> PSU An indefinitely prolonged human inquiry would encounter theoretical conflicts for which it was unable to achieve permanent weak resolutions.

Informally PSU is the thesis that our capacity to pose general questions outruns our capacity to resolve them. PSU is unambiguously at odds with the claim that human inquiry has an unlimited capacity to resolve general questions, so its credentials are of great interest to us.

I have suggested that the customary formulations, strong and weak, of the underdetermination thesis are inadequate, failing as they do to take account of the theory dependence of evidence and evidential support. Many of the specific examples, however, that have been offered in support of the weak and strong underdetermination theses in the large literature provide apparent support for their pragmatic counterparts. Similarly, certain general arguments that have been thought to lead to WU and SU are apparently conducive to PWU and PSU. Let us first review some of these arguments.

Radical underdetermination of theory by data is sometimes presented as the claim that theory is underdetermined by 'all possible observations (evidence or data)'.[2] This is surely to be construed as an abbreviation of a claim of the form: 'For all finite bodies of evidence E, ...' But if the expression 'all possible evidence' is taken to denote a set of items of evidence, the way is open to the following line of thought. Take any body of evidence E. There will always be inconsistent theories T, T' that are compatible with E. This is merely the trivial underdetermination thesis that theories 'go beyond' the data. Normally we can still hope to resolve the issue strongly (that is, refute one or both theories) by considering more evidence. But if E is the totality of possible evidence, then no such resolution can be hoped for. As it stands this unprepossessing argument yields only WU, but it can be modified to yield SU by substituting as a premiss the stronger but still fairly uncontentious thesis that for any given body of evidence E there exist theories T, T' equally well supported by E. It is obvious that corresponding 'arguments' for PWU and PSU could be contrived. Once explicitly displayed, such attempts to parlay trivial underdetermination of theory by evidence into a radical underdetermination thesis are exposed as frauds; for it is absurd to consider all possible evidence as a definite totality.

Another and much more insidious line of argument that attempts to extort a radical underdetermination thesis from an uncontentious form of underdetermination is as follows. Quine, following Duhem, has famously argued that 'any statement can be held true come what may, provided we make drastic enough adjustments elsewhere in the system'. The Duhem–Quine thesis may be thought to warrant the claim that it is always possible to hang on to a scientific theory come what may in the way of anomalies, provided we are prepared to make repeated adjustments in the auxiliary hypotheses that relate the theory to a domain of evidence, and in the background theories relative to which the domain of relevant evidence is defined.[3] Suppose now that there are inconsistent but equally well-supported theories in some domain. If both can be everlastingly rescued from falsification by repeated adjustments in auxiliary hypotheses, there is, so it seems, no prospect of a strong resolution; and since the theories are equally well supported, no prospect of a weak resolution either.

The case for strong underdetermination here is spurious. For there is no reason to suppose that the adjustments to auxiliary hypotheses needed to preserve the conflicting theories will themselves be equally well supported by the available evidence. But the degree of support of the auxiliary hypotheses associated with a theory surely reflects on the extent to which the theory itself is supported.

This case for the weak underdetermination thesis is harder to assess.[4] Much depends upon the way in which units of appraisal are defined. If the units are taken to be fully articulated theories, no case for the pragmatic version of the thesis emerges. Here the adjustments made to escape anomalies cannot be made in the auxiliary hypotheses that relate the central postulates of the theory to its domains of evidence and application, because those hypotheses are already included in the theory. If a theory, in this sense, is to be rescued, it will have to be done by making adjustments in the background theories relative to which its domain of

[3] Lakatos's claim about the irrefutability of the 'hard-cores' of research programmes provides a well-known instance of such an application of the Duhem–Quine thesis: 'Falsificationism and the methodology of scientific research programmes', in I. Lakatos and A. Musgrave, eds., *Criticism and the Growth of Knowledge*, Cambridge, 1970, 91–196.

[4] W. V. O. Quine, 'On empirically equivalent systems of the world', *Erkenntnis*, 9 (1975), 313–28, p. 313, suggests that the Duhem–Quine thesis 'lends credence to the [empirical] underdetermination theses'; the theses he refers to are, in our sense, weak ones.

relevant evidence is defined. But this possibility does not impinge on PWU, which is concerned with refutation of theories relative to sets of background theories that are not, at the times in question, up for revision.

Suppose, on the other hand, that the units of appraisal are taken to be not fully articulated theories but rather sets of central postulates, the 'hard cores' of Lakatosian research programmes. Then we do have the makings of a serious case for PWU. Such theories can, it may be suggested, be rescued from anomalies without modifying the background theories relative to which the domain of relevant evidence is defined, by making adjustments in the auxiliary hypotheses which connect the theory with its domain of evidence. In many instances of theoretical conflict this suggestion seems rather implausible. Consider, for example, the clash between Mendelian genetics and Galtonian genetics or that between fixist and continental drift accounts of the earth's crustal history, clashes that may well be regarded as conflicts of research programmes. In each of these cases the set of background theories involved in determination of the domain of relevant evidence is vast, ranging over many fields of inquiry. But it is far from clear that the Duhem–Quine thesis allows the privileged subset of beliefs to be preserved in the face of anomalies to constitute a substantial proportion of the total consensus, leaving the 'adjustments elsewhere' to be carried out in the narrow compass of auxiliary hypotheses that relate a theory to its domain of evidence. The suggestion becomes more plausible, however, not when we consider conflicts that take place against backgrounds of at least tacit agreement over a wide range of theories, but when we consider near global conflicts of paradigms or world-pictures—corpuscular mechanism vs. Aristotelian physics, the Newtonian world-picture vs. the Cartesian world-picture, etc. Here the balance between background theories and auxiliary hypotheses is apparently shifted, the range of neutral background theories being relatively small, the range of auxiliary hypotheses needed to connect the core postulates to their domains of evidence being very large. There is here ample room for the 'adjustments elsewhere' needed to preserve the rival theories come what may in the face of anomalies. Serious doubt, however, will shortly be cast on the occurrence of such near global conflicts.

Let us now consider a couple of supposed recipes for generating instances of underdetermination of theory by data. The first may be called 'vacuous expansion'. Take a theory T. Extend T to T' and T'' using inconsistent but empirically vacuous hypotheses.[5] T' and T'', being empirically equivalent to T, will be empirically equivalent. Typical strategies for the construction of such vacuous expansions include postulation of agencies or mechanisms whose effects cancel each other and postulation of agencies or mechanisms whose effects are undetectable by any physically possible measurement device. Though there is room for doubt about the intelligibility of some such postulates, the demonstrability of PWU by this means must, I think, be conceded. Vacuous expansion cannot, however, be used to instantiate PSU. For a theory is surely better supported by its evidence than is any vacuous expansion of it. So weak resolution of a conflict between vacuous expansions T', T'' of a theory T may always be achieved by retreat to T.

The second recipe is equally straightforward. Take a theory T and pick out the theoretical predicates that are peculiar to it. Now construct a new theory T' by uniformly permuting some or all of those predicates, whilst keeping their references constant. Here, it seems, both PWU and PSU are instantiated. For T and T' are inconsistent; and they will not only be compatible with exactly the same evidence, but also—unless mere choice of notation can affect the support of a theory—equally well supported by any given body of evidence. This kind of example is commonly dismissed on the grounds that isomorphism of the kind induced by such a permutation of terms is a sufficient condition for theoretical identity.[6] But this response fails to explain why it is not legitimate to appeal to the preservation of a referential scheme in this context.

The very general objections voiced earlier against notions of correspondence with 'the real world' do, I think, show the illegitimacy of the appeal to a referential scheme that is involved in

---

[5] M. Wilson, 'The observational uniqueness of some theories', *The Journal of Philosophy*, 77 (1980), 208–33, pp. 217–19, and Quine, 'On empirically equivalent systems', p. 323, discuss such cases and mention examples that have been presented as serious instances of underdetermination; both treat them as trivial, suggesting that an interesting underdetermination thesis should explicitly exclude them.

[6] Various forms of isomorphism are presented as sufficient conditions of theoretical identity by C. Glymour, 'Theoretical realism and theoretical equivalence', in R. C. Buck and R. S. Cohen, *Boston Studies in the Philosophy of Science*, 8 (1970), 275–88, pp. 279–80; W. Newton-Smith, 'The underdetermination of theory by data', *Proceedings of the Aristotelian Society*, supplementary vol. 52 (1978), 71–91, p. 78; Quine, 'On empirically equivalent systems', 319–20; and Wilson, 'The observational uniqueness of some theories', p. 217.

these alleged instances of underdetermination. But a more specific *ad hominem* objection may be raised against this particular piece of world-mongering. It is surely a condition of adequacy for an account of reference that it entail the impossibility of all our beliefs about things of a given kind being false, but true of things of some other kind.[7] So a theory obtained by permuting the theoretical terms of a theory we believe whilst keeping the referential scheme constant can be ruled out as false a priori. The view, however, that there exist theories isomorphic to our own and empirically indiscernible from them, but eliminable a priori as false, is bizarre. Rather than concede this bizarrerie we should refuse to admit the coherence of the supposition that terms of a theory may be permuted whilst their referents remain unchanged. Once the incoherence of the claim about preservation of reference is admitted, it does indeed become obvious that a theory generated by such permutation of terms is a mere notational variant.

These two recipes, the 'vacuous expansion' recipe and the 'permutation' recipe, fail to produce instances of permanently irresoluble theoretical conflicts of the kind needed to substantiate the pragmatic strong underdetermination thesis. The first recipe fails because the rival theories it generates are not distinct enough— the conflict can always be resolved by retreating to the base theory by whose inflation the rivals were created. The second fails because it does not in fact generate distinct theories.

Having failed to substantiate any threatening form of underdetermination by appeal to recipes for the contrivance of artificial examples, let us consider some putative real examples of underdetermination suggested by the history or the current state of the sciences.

First, there is the intriguing possibility that the theories we now hold (or are on the verge of holding) may entail the empirical underdetermination of certain theoretical issues. Current physical theory places definite constraints on the accessibility to observers in a given spatio-temporal region of information about states of affairs in other spatio-temporal regions. Glymour has shown that, given these constraints, certain pairs of cosmological theories T, T' are related as follows: if T then, given our situation in the universe, no matter how prolonged (and well-travelled) our investigations, we

---

[7] Cf. Horwich, 'How to choose between empirically indistinguishable theories', 66–8.

cannot hope to resolve the issue between T and T' by a crucial observation.[8] Malament has elaborated Glymour's idea. He argues, convincingly in my cosmologically untutored judgement, that this may well be the cosmologist's predicament.[9] In that case at least PWU is confirmed by our current physical theories. Malament also considers the extent to which such empirically indiscernible cosmological theories are invariant with respect to global properties of space-time.[10] His results are apt to discourage the view that weak resolutions of the issues between such theories could always be achieved by appeal to considerations of cosmological simplicity. Perhaps PSU is confirmed as well.[11]

The instances of underdetermination adduced by Glymour and Malament are essentially 'internal': they concern questions that arise in the context of a background theory that both specifies the types of evidence that would resolve them and shows that evidence to be inaccessible. A second type of putative instances of under-determination of theory is, if substantiated, far more dramatic in its implications, concerning as it does certain global clashes of paradigms, world-pictures, etc., that have allegedly enlivened the history of science.

An apparently very strong case can be made for holding that clashes of world-pictures—corpuscular mechanism vs. Aristotelian physics, Cartesian vs. Newtonian cosmology, etc.—exemplify the pragmatic strong underdetermination thesis. To start with it may be pointed out that in such global or near global conflicts the identifica-tion of 'neutral' background theories that determine the body of evidence germane to the conflict becomes problematic. The most aggressive line of attack on this score is that which maintains that in some, at least, of these global conflicts no neutral background theories whatsoever are to be found. At the end of the last chapter it was suggested, on grounds connected with the principle of human-ity of interpretation, that we cannot coherently envisage such all-encompassing conflicts. Further, whatever the superficial appeal of the notion that contact with alien inquirers might involve us in such

[8] C. Glymour, 'Topology, cosmology and convention', *Synthese*, 24 (1972), 195–218; 'Indistinguishable space-times and the fundamental group', in J. S. Earman *et al.*, eds., *Minnesota Studies in the Philosophy of Science*, 8 (1977), 50–60.

[9] D. Malament, 'Observationally indistinguishable space-times', in Earman *et al.*, eds., *Minnesota Studies*, 61–79.

[10] Ibid., 70–4.

[11] I am indebted to Jeremy Butterfield for pointing this out to me.

a total theoretical conflict, the claim that the history of human science has involved conflicts of this sort is most implausible. More moderately it may be suggested that conflicts of world-pictures have occurred in which the set of neutral background theories has been very restricted: sufficiently restricted to render weak (and *a fortiori* strong) resolution unattainable. There are a number of telling ways in which the plausibility of this suggestion may be enhanced. We have already noted how the Duhem–Quine thesis may be used to support the claim that each of the conflicting world-pictures could be preserved come what may in the face of anomalies by making adjustments in the extensive collection of auxiliary hypotheses needed to relate abstract and general postulates to concrete evidence. Alternatively, one may follow Kuhn and Feyerabend in emphasizing the opportunist and 'irrational' means of persuasion that were in fact used to win adherents to world-pictures.[12] The widespread deployment of such stratagems is symptomatic, it may be urged, of the unavailability of genuinely reliable criteria of sufficient power to resolve such near global conflicts.

Our rebuttal of the argument for underdetermination from clashes of world-pictures consists in a straightforward denial of the occurrence of such clashes. The paradigmatic clashes of world-pictures—Aristotelian physics vs. corpuscular mechanism, the Newtonian vs. the Cartesian world-picture—were not, we shall maintain, the near global conflicts that they are widely said to have been. First, it may be pointed out that certain quite explicit bodies of theory were not called in question by these conflicts; obvious examples are elementary statics and geometrical optics, the latter being a theory whose importance in underwriting a domain of empirical evidence can scarcely be exaggerated. The areas of common ground are greatly enlarged when we consider the various categories of commonplace and common-sensical beliefs about natural phenomena: think, for instance, of the enormous body of generalizations about celestial phenomena that remained undisturbed in the seventeenth-century clash of world-systems or of the vast body of generalizations about the manifest properties of natural kinds of plants and animals that remained beyond dispute in

[12] P. K. Feyerabend, *Against Method: Outline of an Anarchistic Theory of Knowledge*, London, 1975, especially chs. 11 and 12. T. S. Kuhn, *The Essential Tension*, Chicago, 1977, 320–39.

the clash between fixist and evolutionist paradigms. Appreciation of yet further reaches of common ground is gained when we consider the various types of tacit and unacknowledged beliefs. Here belongs the host of implicit beliefs that underlie practical and technological activities; and here too belongs the whole range of entrenched but inarticulate beliefs about the means and proper objects of inquiry that are constitutive of the disciplines within which conflict occurs.

The 'catastrophist' image is one of wholesale confrontation followed by rapid triumph of one world-picture over its rival in all its various domains of application. But when we look at the historical details of such alleged catastrophies a quite different picture emerges, one of piecemeal confrontation and piecemeal resolution of conflict taking place in a variety of domains, often with very different time-scales.[13] Foreshortening of the historical time-scale through lack of attention to the detailed chronology of conflict, over-much concentration on dramatic triumphs of paradigm in particular fields, simplification for didactic purposes, and, above all, the tendency to focus on 'winners' and to write off 'losers' once the first symptoms of their weakness have appeared—all conspire to conceal the protracted and piecemeal character of scientific revolutions.

By way of example, take the celebrated conflict of Cartesian and Newtonian world-pictures. This particular conflict has a number of features that should commend it to the promoter of under-determination theses. There can be no doubt in this instance that protagonists of the rival world-pictures entered into controversy. In this respect it contrasts, for example, with the alleged confrontation of Aristotelian physics with corpuscular mechanism, a confrontation which it is surprisingly difficult to substantiate by adducing actual controversies prosecuted under the aegis of the rival paradigms. Further, the range of domains of inquiry in which the rival world-pictures confronted each other is, in this instance, impressively wide—the various domains of physics (optics, celestial dynamics, magnetics, etc.), cosmogony, meteorology, physiology ('animal economy'), and so on. In this respect it constrasts markedly with the many clashes of paradigms that were tied to

---

[13] Much material for a defence of this kind of interpretation of scientific revolutions is provided by I. B. Cohen, *Revolution in Science*, Cambridge, Mass., 1985.

single fields, Ptolemaic vs. Copernican cosmology and Stahlian vs. Lavoisierian chemistry, for example. Finally, it is a clash that involved world-pictures whose content can be specified precisely enough for the question of the adequacy of the means that were (or could have been) used to resolve it to be tackled.[14] In this respect it contrasts with clashes of paradigms in which one or both paradigms had contents of a kind resistant to full and precise articulation; for example, the sixteenth-century clash between 'orthodox' and Paracelsian medicine.

A consideration of the fortunes of the Cartesian system, from its inception to its gradual collapse in the third and fourth decades of the eighteenth century, fails to reveal across-the-board confrontation with other world-pictures. Rather, debates about the credentials of Cartesianism developed fairly independently and with very different time-scales in the fields of metaphysics, physics, chemistry cosmogony, meteorology, and physiology.[15] Even within physics, the main locus of conflict with Newtonian doctrines, no single general conflict occurred; rather, the debates whose outcomes were eventually to seal the fate of Cartesian physics were, on the whole, localized within its subdisciplines, optics, celestial mechanics, theory of impact, study of magnetism, study of electricity, study of 'fire', etc.[16] Further, it should be noted that however extensive the

---

[14] However, it has recently been convincingly argued that the doctrinal homogeneity of Newtonian and Cartesian natural philosophy has been exaggerated: see S. Schaffer, 'Natural philosophy', in G. S. Rousseau and R. Porter, eds., *The Ferment of Knowledge. Studies in the Historiography of Eighteenth-Century Science*, Cambridge, 1980, 55–91, and J. L. Heilbron, 'Experimental natural philosophy', ibid., 357–87.

[15] On the fortunes of Cartesian physics see R. Dugas, *La Mécanique au XVIIe siècle*, Neuchâtel, 1954, ch. IX; P. Mouy, *Le développement de la physique Cartésienne, 1646–1712*, Paris, 1934; P. Brunet, *L'introduction des théories de Newton en France au XVIIIe siècle. Tome 1: Avant 1738*, Paris, 1931; E. G. Ruestow, *Physics at Seventeenth and Eighteenth Century Leiden: Philosophy and the New Science in the University*, The Hague, 1973. The literature on the metaphysical debates occasioned by Cartesianism is vast. The fortunes of Cartesian physiology are retailed by T. M. Brown, *The Mechanical Philosophy and the 'Animal Oeconomy'*, New York, 1981. The fortunes of Cartesian cosmogony are explored by J. Roger, 'The Cartesian model and its role in eighteenth-century "theory of the earth" ', in T. M. Lennon et al., *Problems of Cartesianism*, Montreal, 1982, 95–112.

[16] In addition to the works cited above, see, e.g., A. I. Sabra, *Theories of Light from Descartes to Newton*, Cambridge, 1967; G. Cantor, *Optics after Newton. Theories of Light in Britain and Ireland, 1704–1840*, Manchester, 1984; E. J. Aiton, *The Vortex Theory of Planetary Motions*, London, 1972; R. W. Home, ' "Newtonianism" and the theory of the magnet', *History of Science*, 15 (1977), 252–66.

potential conflict between the systems at the level of explanatory hypotheses, a very substantial bulk of mathematical descriptive physics (notably in statics, elementary mechanics, optics, and harmonics) remained uncontentious.[17] In its decline—at the beginning of the eighteenth century in England, a couple of decades later in France—Cartesian physics was indeed attacked across the board from the standpoint of the victorious Newtonian physics;[18] but the Newtonian victory (or, to be accurate, near victory, for the consensus in the mathematical physics of, say, 1750 contained many Cartesian elements) was in fact the product of a multiplicity of skirmishes and campaigns of varied scale and duration fought on many fronts.

To conclude, various arguments for radical underdetermination of theory by data have been reviewed and, for the most part, found unconvincing. A few concessions have, however, been made. The plausibility of PWU, the claim that there are theoretical conflicts that we could never permanently resolve by crucial experiment, has been conceded for trivial conflicts generated by vacuous expansion of theories and for 'internal' cosmological issues of the kinds raised by Glymour and Malament. It is PSU, however, the claim that there are theoretical conflicts that we could never permanently resolve by reliable means, that poses a serious threat to scientific absolutism. The plausibility of this has been conceded only for internal cosmological questions. To complete the defence of scientific absolutism against radical underdetermination two further tasks remain. First, we must show that concession of the irresolubility of internal cosmological questions is not a fatal concession; this is attempted in

---

[17] Thus it was possible for English Newtonians to use the Cartesian Jacques Rohault's *Traité de physique* (critically annotated by Samuel Clarke) as a textbook. Similarly, it has been shown by Piers Bursill-Hall that the shift from a commitment to Cartesianism at the University of Paris had little immediate repercussion on the teaching of mathematical physics, since much of the syllabus lay in this uncontentious common ground: 'The teaching of mathematics at the University of Paris in the eighteenth century', unpublished seminar paper delivered at the Department of History and Philosophy of Science, Cambridge, 1984.

[18] The Newtonian Samuel Clarke's notes to his translation of 1710 of Rohault's Cartesian *Traité de physique* (1671) constitute a general attack; but as shown by M. A. Hoskin the two earlier versions of Clarke's notes are much less extensively critical: ' "Mining all within": Clarke's notes to Rohault's *Traité de physique*', *The Thomist*, 24 (1961), 353–63. Similarly, d'Alembert's entry 'Cartésianisme' in the second volume of the *Encyclopédie* (1752), whilst honouring Descartes, dismisses the central tenets of the Cartesian system.

Chapter IX. Secondly and crucially, we must say more about the ways in which the reliability of methods for the resolution of theoretical conflict may be established. That is the task of the next two chapters.

VII

Reliability and Inquiry 1: Calibration

To fend off the threat to scientific absolutism posed by empirical underdetermination of theory strong claims have been made about our capacity to achieve reliable resolutions of theoretical conflicts and about the means by which we may do so. In particular, it has been claimed that we have the capacity to arrive at reliable resolutions of conflicts even when no 'crucial experiment' is forthcoming; and it has been suggested that the methods and criteria of theory assessment used to achieve such resolutions are often local in their application and sensitive to theoretical context. If our case against the existence of irresoluble theoretical conflicts is to carry conviction, more must be said about the ways in which the reliabilities of such methods may be established.

Our pragmatic account of truth is not entirely devoid of implications for the conduct of inquiries directed towards the attainment of truth. Thus the account ties the notion of truth to that of the eventual verdicts of certain sequences of sets of consistent beliefs. The attempt to overcome inconsistencies, for example those that arise from conflict of theory-based predictions with perceptual judgements, is thus enjoined on seekers after truth. Further, the hypothetical series of total theories in terms of whose eventual verdicts truth is defined exhibit the properties of infinite resolution of questions, infinite transcendence of error, and absolute dominance. The links of truth with resolution of questions, transcendence of error, and domination of other inquiries are such as to enjoin on seekers after truth the attempts, respectively, to answer or dissolve outstanding questions, to track down and root out sources of error, and to resolve conflicts between their own theories and those of other inquirers. Despite these exceedingly general constraints on the conduct of truth-directed inquiries, however, our account does not have specific normative implications for the assessment of theories: if methods are to be warranted as reliable, the warrants will have to be a posteriori.

Before considering ways of establishing a posteriori the reliability of methods and criteria, certain very general objections to naturalistic approaches to epistemology deserve mention. First, there is the charge that the project of a posteriori justification of methods of theory assessment presupposes the possibility of regimenting the endlessly various and context-dependent 'good reasons' that may be invoked for this purpose into a general and universally binding canon of scientific method.[1] Secondly, there is the charge that a posteriori attempts to warrant the reliabilities of methods are irredeemably circular.[2] Thirdly, and closely related to the circularity charge, there is the objection that because it fails to engage in the central project of traditional epistemology, that of defeating the radical sceptic, such a posteriori or naturalized epistemology is unworthy of the title 'epistemology'.[3]

The first of the objections is relatively easily met. Naturalized epistemology of the kind to be endorsed here aims to show how in the course of ongoing scientific inquiries particular methods for the evaluation of evidence and the assessment of theories may be shown a posteriori to be reliable. It is in no way committed to a project of formulation and justification of a complete canon of scientific method: rather the discovery of reliable methods and criteria and the making out of cases for the reliabilities of methods are envisaged as open-ended activities, part and parcel of the various enterprises of scientific inquiry themselves.[4]

The second objection is more pressing. Certainly it must be conceded that if circularity is to be avoided, there are precautions to be taken in justifying methods a posteriori. For example, an a posteriori case for the reliability of method M must not depend on premises that are seriously called in question when the reliability of

---

[1] H. Putnam, for example, attacks naturalized epistemology on this score: 'Why reason can't be naturalized', *Synthese*, 52 (1982), 3–37.

[2] R. Firth, for example, argues that attempts to justify what we take to be criteria of rational acceptability by appeal to their reliability as guides to truth are inescapably circular, because those very criteria provide our only way of identifying truths: 'Epistemic merit, intrinsic and instrumental', *Proceedings and Addresses of the American Philosophical Association*, 55 (1981), 5–23, pp. 18–21. Putnam, 'Why reason can't be naturalized', p. 5, apparently endorses this argument. A telling riposte to Firth is J. Heil, 'Reliability and epistemic merit', *Australasian Journal of Philosophy*, 62 (1984), 327–38.

[3] The charge is levelled against naturalized epistemology by Richard Rorty, *Philosophy and the Mirror of Nature*, Princeton, 1979, 221–30.

[4] Explicit assumption by the sciences of the tasks of legitimating their own rules of procedure is presented by J.-F. Lyotard as the mark of 'post-modernity': *La condition postmoderne*, Paris, 1979, 51–2, 89–90.

M is called in question. Further, the case for the reliability of M must not involve an application of M itself. Provided such precautions are observed, it is hard to see on what grounds a general charge of circularity against a posteriori justifications can be sustained.

These precautions against circularity do, however, reveal the justice of at least one version of the third charge. Were a global conflict of world-pictures to arise it would be impossible to provide non-circular a posteriori justification for any method by which the conflict might be resolved. One way of interpreting the sceptic's appeals to malicious demons and malevolent neuro-surgeons is precisely as attempts to adumbrate world-pictures in global conflict with our own. If radical scepticism is to be countered, other means will have to be found. To concede that naturalized epistemology cannot refute radical scepticism, however, is by no means to concede its inefficacy against the cases for scepticism on specific theoretical issues that arise from putative instances of underdetermination of theory.

With these preliminary defensive remarks off our chests, let us turn to the main question of this chapter: How is it possible to show a posteriori that methods of theory assessment are reliable?

One pattern of a posteriori justification has already been indicated in passing. Methods of theory assessment that apply to relatively local theoretical questions posed against substantial backgrounds of uncontentious theory may often be justified by appeal to those background theories. Consider the stipulation that in assessing hypotheses about the impact on plant distributions of changes in the disposition of land masses little weight should be attached to past or present distributions of spore-bearing plants or to those of the lighter seeded flowering plants. The stipulation is justified a posteriori by appeal to direct evidence for the aerial transport of spores and by appeal to theoretical studies of the transport of bodies in turbulent airstreams such as the trade winds. Or, to take another example mentioned earlier, consider the injunction not to treat exhaustiveness in the assignment of functions to morphological features as prerequisite for an adequate account of the adaptation of a type of organism to its environment. The justification here is that certain features of organisms may be a 'spin-off' of developmental processes that give rise to other features that are adaptive, rather than being adaptive features in their own right; and this, in turn, is an assumption that can be justified by appeal to well-confirmed generalizations about the nature of developmental processes in organisms and about the processes of organic evolution.

Justifications of this homely sort are, however, less likely to be available in cases where extensive theoretical conflict greatly reduces the range of uncontentious background theories that can be appealed to, or in which the novelty of the theoretical questions posed is such as to render available background theories largely irrelevant to their resolution. In seeking to elucidate further modes of a posteriori justification of methods of theory assessment I shall proceed indirectly, considering first the question of justification of methods for the assessment of evidence in the hope of finding useful analogies.

Let us start by considering criteria for the proper application of measurement procedures. Such criteria may be grouped into two rough-and-ready classes. On the one hand there are criteria which relate to questions of appropriateness of types of measurement procedures: Was the procedure of a type suitable to the object measured? Is the procedure employed sufficiently accurate over the range of values reported?, etc. On the other hand, there are criteria which relate to questions of adequacy of performance of particular measurements: Was the instrument properly aligned? Were proper controls used to minimize interference effects?, etc. To bring the issues involved in the justification of such criteria down to earth let us consider a specific example.[5] (Readers entirely unfamiliar with chemistry may find this example unilluminating; those with a smattering of physics will find the main points to be made here nicely illustrated in Ian Hacking's account of the operation of PEGGY II, a device for measuring departures from parity in the scattering of polarized electrons from deuterium.[6])

SDS–PAGE (Sodium Dodecyl Sulphate Polyacrylamide Gel Electrophoresis) is the most widely used technique for estimating the molecular weights of polypeptides, the molecular subunits of proteins. The majority of proteins when heated at $100°C$ in the

---

[5] The following account is largely based on B. D. Hames, 'An introduction to polyacrylamide gel electrophoresis', and A. Chrambach and D. Rodband, ' "Quantitative" and preparative polyacrylamide gel electrophoresis', both in B. D. Hames and D. Rickwood, eds., *Gel Electrophoresis of Proteins: A Practical Approach*, London, 1981.

[6] I. Hacking, *Representing and Intervening: Introductory Topics in the Philosophy of Science*, Cambridge, 1983, 266–73.

presence of the ionic detergent sodium dodecyl sulphate are dissoci-
ated into their component polypeptides. The polypeptide subunits
bond with SDS in a constant weight ratio to form complexes that are
approximately spherical and of roughly constant highly negative
charge. The mobility of the SDS-polypeptide complex under
electrophoresis (that is, migrating under the influence of a potential
gradient) through a polyacrylamide gel is determined by the molecular weight of the polypeptide, the gel acting as a 'molecular sieve'.
By using marker polypeptides of known molecular weights under
the same electrophoretic conditions as the sample, the molecular
weight of the sample polypeptide can be estimated.

Criteria of appropriateness for the use of SDS–PAGE concern
the chemical types of protein to which the technique is applicable,
the ranges of polypeptide molecular weights over which it is
reliable, and the accuracy of the technique in different parts of its
range. In each case only partial theoretical justifications of the
criteria are available. Thus it is known that the technique does not
work for very large polypeptides, because they clog the gel, and that
it does not work for very small polypeptides, because they slip
through the pores almost frictionlessly; but the precise range of
applicability has to be determined by calibration against
polypeptides of independently determined molecular weights. It is
known too that the procedure is inapplicable to certain proteins
whose polypeptides fail to bond with SDS and to others whose
polypeptides do bond, but form complexes of inconstant weight
ratios or of highly non-spherical shapes. Such anomalies cannot
generally be predicted on theoretical grounds, but are rather
discovered by trial and error. Similarly, although theoretically
based predictions of a qualitative sort can be made about some of
the factors which affect the sensitivity of SDS–PAGE, determination of error bounds is entirely an experimental matter involving
calibration against polypeptides of known molecular weights. For
certain other criteria of adequacy of performance the role of
underlying theory is more substantial. For example, the effective-
ness of the procedure depends crucially on the choice of buffer
system. This is an issue of quite extraordinary complexity, especially when discontinuous buffer systems (which allow preliminary
sorting of polypeptide species prior to resolution in the 'sieving' gel)
are used. In the early days of the technique design of buffer systems
was a matter of rule of thumb and trial and error; but the general

theory of moving boundaries has now been developed to a stage where it is possible in the case of certain types of apparatuses to predict (with the help of the computer) optimal buffer systems.

Molecular weight determination by SDS–PAGE is, I suggest, a typical scientific measurement procedure with respect to the ways in which conditions for reliable application are established. The extents to which we possess theoretical understanding of the workings of measurement procedures and of the conditions for their application vary very widely. At one extreme we have simple and long-established instruments—the beam balance and the ammeter, for example—of whose workings we have a fairly complete theoretical understanding. In such instances conditions for reliable application can, on the whole, be justified by appeal to theoretical accounts of the ways in which the instruments work. But even here, though underlying theory provides bounds on ranges of reliable application and on sensitivity in different parts of the range, detailed estimates require calibrations of instruments against standards. At the other extreme lie new and complex procedures whose detailed workings are scarcely understood—that was the position with SDS–PAGE 15 years ago. In such cases the establishment of conditions of reliable application is almost entirely derived by calibration against standards. Typical measurement procedures such as SDS–PAGE and use of PEGGY II lie between the two extremes, understanding of the conditions for their reliable deployment depending in part on theoretical analysis of the instruments employed and in part on experimental calibration, trial and error, and rule of thumb.[7]

Now let us consider, rather perfunctorily, criteria for assessment of evidence gained by direct observation, the 'testimony of the senses'. Again, a single specific example will be considered. Judgement of distance is chosen on the grounds that it has long been a major focus of psychological research and is a topic on which there have been major achievements.[8] Here relatively simple criteria of appropriateness concern the ranges and accuracies of judgements made on objects of varied sizes under varied lighting conditions.

    [7] The substantial roles of tacit know-how and trained 'instinct' in the debugging and competent use of measurement devices is well documented by Hacking, *Representing and Intervening*, chs. 9–16.

    [8] On perception of depth and distance see, e.g., R. L. Gregory, *Eye and Brain*, 3rd rev. edn., London, 1977, 64–75, and D. Marr, *Vision*, San Francisco, 1982, 111–59.

More complex criteria of appropriateness concern the effects on distance judgements of relative motions of various kinds and the various special circumstances that may give rise to relative distance 'illusions'. Criteria of performance include those which have to do with the proper functioning of the eye as an optimal instrument as well as those which concern post-retinal neural function. The injunction to mistrust judgements of distance by persons with astigmatism belongs to the former category; to the latter category belongs the injunction to mistrust the judgements of distance by persons whose visual cortex is damaged. As in the case of criteria of adequacy of measurement, the types of justification turn out to be varied. Some criteria can be given partial theoretical justifications. Thus the injunction to distrust judgements of objects' relative distances when the observer and the objects have remained quite stationary can be given a partial justification in terms of parallax and the optics of the eye. Similarly, recent work on post-retinal mechanisms of stereopsis provides theoretical justification (of an admittedly highly conjectural nature) for criteria relating to depth illusions, notably those that arise from 'illusory outlines' generated by the filling in of unlikely gaps in the course of post-retinal processing. Justification of detailed and effective criteria for assessment of distance judgements, however, would require trial-and-error calibration of observers under varied conditions.

Generalization from two instances plucked from an enormous field is a risky business. However, certain general features of methods for the assessment of evidence—both evidence arising from use of measurement instruments and that based on use of the unaided senses—are, I suggest, fairly uncontentious.

1. In using measurement instruments, as in using the unaided senses, competence depends largely on tacit knowledge.

2. Methods for assessing the soundness of evidence are, for the most part, both local in their domains of application and at least implicitly theoretical context-dependent. There are, to be sure, a few generally applicable criteria—for example, the injunction to distrust reports of measurements performed using apparatus that is very dirty or is delivering signals beset by 'noise'. But such general criteria are few and far between, impracticably vague, and liable to many exceptions. Equally there are some criteria of adequacy of performance—distrust results of beam balance measurements in

which the plumb line was not vertical—that, whilst doubtless in principle sensitive to theoretical context, may be considered to be theoretical context-free for most practical purposes. But the majority of criteria are manifestly tied in their application to particular types of measurement procedures and are obviously (if not explicitly) answerable to theoretical considerations.

3. The contrast that is sometimes drawn between scientific measurement instruments as devices whose workings we understand, and human perceptual mechanisms as devices whose workings we do not understand, is thoroughly misleading. In both cases background theories tend to be insufficient to justify the currently available criteria for appropriate application and proper use. In particular, criteria of adequacy concerned with range and accuracy of measurement and observation procedures, criteria vital in almost all scientific applications of our senses and measurement instruments, can generally be justified only by testing the procedures against objects whose relevant properties are established on independent grounds: that is, by calibration against standards.

4. Calibration against standards can show that a measurement or perceptual procedure is reliable when applied in certain ways to certain types of objects or systems. It cannot, however, explain such reliability. An alternative way of demonstrating reliability is through theoretical analysis. The task of such theoretical analysis is to show that under proper conditions of use the output of the device under consideration is so causally constrained by its input as to render that output a reliable indicator of the relevant state of the object or system to which the device is applied. In the case of measurement instruments such explanations depend upon the establishment of causal chains originating in the objects or systems measured, proceeding via internal states of the measurement device and eventuating in readings of the instrument—causal chains so specified as to show why bounds on the values of the relevant parameters of the objects or systems measured can be reliably inferred from those readings. Analogously in the case of perception such explanations will depend on the establishment of causal chains originating in the objects perceived, proceeding via states of the medium of perception and states of the sense organs, and eventuating in perceptual judgements—causal chains so specified as to show why the perceptual judgement is reliably indicative of the relevant

state of the perceived object.[9] Calibration of measurement and perceptual methods can provide only 'surface' justification, showing that certain procedures are reliable, but not why they are reliable. This kind of theoretical analysis, however, aims at 'deep' justification, which shows at once that and why procedures are reliable.

Now let us consider the extent to which these generalizations about methods for the assessment of evidence can be transposed to methods for the assessment of theories. Transposition of the first two generalizations is unproblematic. It is uncontroversial to claim that competent assessment of theories is to some extent guided by tacit knowledge, by 'feel', by 'instinct', etc., of types resistant to codification. Nor is it questionable that many widely used methods of theory assessment are both local and theoretical context-dependent in their applications.

The ready transposibility of the first two generalizations provides modest grounds for optimism on the more problematic, and for our purposes more interesting, question of the existence of analogues at the level of theory assessment to the establishment of the reliability of measurement and perceptual procedures by calibration and theoretical analysis.

It is relatively easy to develop the analogy in the case of justification by calibration. Such justification of a method or criterion for theory assessment is obtained by showing that its application tends to favour theories whose truth is warranted on independent grounds. The following discussion will be restricted to the special case of methods for resolution of theoretical conflict. The general pattern for calibration of methods for the resolution of theoretical conflict will be as follows. Suppose that T conflicts with T' and that there are grounds independent of the reliability of M for holding T to be true, or a better approximation to the truth than T'; then if M applied to the conflict between T and T' adjudicates in favour of T, the reliability of M is confirmed. We shall shortly consider some of

[9] The claim that perception involves the selective picking up of information about objects that is afforded by the various kinds of physical stimulation is central to J. J. Gibson's perceptual psychology: see, e.g., *The Senses Considered as Perceptual Systems*, Boston, 1966. Recent philosophical accounts of perception which emphasize the causal processes by which information about perceived objects may be conveyed by and extracted from physical stimuli include U. Neisser, *Cognition and Reality*, San Francisco, 1976, F. I. Dretske, *Knowledge and the Flow of Information*, Cambridge, Mass., 1981, ch. 6, and J. Heil, *Perception and Cognition*, Berkeley, 1983.

the ways in which this scheme of 'surface' justification may be applied in practice.

The question of the existence of analogies to the justification of measurement and perceptual procedures by theoretical analysis is far more problematic. One line along which one may envisage such 'deep' justifications at the level of methods for the resolution of theoretical questions is as follows. Causal explanations would be offered that exhibited users of the methods justified as sensitive detectors of theoretical states of affairs. The explanations would invoke causal processes originating in the theoretical states of affairs, eventuating in beliefs, and mediated by states of the sense organs and brains of inquirers—the causal processes being so specified as to show the contents of the eventual states, consensual beliefs, to be reliably diagnostic for the initial theoretical states of affairs. This programme has many attractions, not least the prospect it opens up of an account of the growth of scientific knowledge as a natural process. It faces, however, a host of problems. The attractions and problems of the programme, as well as the consequences for scientific absolutism should it fail, are discussed in the next chapter.

Let us return to the matter of the establishment of the reliability of methods of theory assessment through calibration. What sorts of theoretical conflicts can be used as standards against which methods of theory assessment may in practice be tested? When the methods of assessment at issue apply to low-level theoretical questions it is often relatively easy to find or contrive standard conflicts. One may, for example, appeal to recently resolved controversies. Thus the claim that palaeomagnetic evidence is of greater weight than biogeographical evidence in resolving general questions about the crustal history of the earth may be confirmed by pointing out that where biogeographical evidence is equivocal, palaeomagnetic evidence strongly favours the continental drift hypothesis against the continental fixity hypothesis—a conflict that was decisively settled in favour of continental drift by a third kind of data, namely sea-floor magnetic anomalies.[10] Alternatively, the reliability of a method may be confirmed by an appeal to standards cooked up on the spot. Consider the injunction to distrust hypotheses about the

---

[10] On the implications of palaeomagnetism for continental drift see, e.g., A. Hallam, *A Revolution in the Earth Sciences: From Continental Drift to Plate Tectonics*, Oxford, 1973, 38–43.

locations of cerebral functions that are based only on correlations between brain damage and behavioural malfunction. This is readily justified by adducing some of the many absurd hypotheses, entirely at odds with current understanding of the anatomy and physiology of the brain, that would appear warranted were we to attach undue weight to such correlations.

When, however, we look for standard conflicts against which to test the reliability of methods for the resolution of larger-scale theoretical conflicts, this routine and homely approach becomes on several counts problematic. Only in the liveliest fields of inquiry will recent scientific debates yield a sufficient variety of theories radically different from those that command the current consensus. Moreover, serious dificulties lie in the way of attempts to augment the stock of standard conflicts by cooking up *de novo* theories very different from our own. For not any theory that conflicts substantially with our own will be adequate for this purpose: it must in addition, if it is to provide a sensitive test, be a theory that does at least passably well by other criteria—not too well, of course, otherwise we might be landed with a serious contender for our allegiance and would no longer be able to assume the correctness of our own theories as a premiss in the calibration. But contrivance of such theories, though obviously not impossible, would require enormous imaginative effort and ingenuity. Further, there would often be serious problems in the application of methods to such imaginary conflicts, problems arising from the need to determine the range of background theories unaffected by the conflict and to establish a domain of 'neutral' evidence. Whilst these difficulties do not absolutely preclude the testing of methods of theory choice against contrived large-scale conflicts, they do provide a powerful incentive to seek elsewhere for large-scale standard conflicts.

In the history of science the hard work of contriving rival hypotheses, rival theories, and rival research programmes has in effect already been done for us. It constitutes a virtually inexhaustible source of standard conflicts of various types and extents. Further, the historical record of the methods and criteria that were in fact employed by protagonists of the rivals will often provide valuable guides to the selection of conflicts appropriate for testing the reliability of particular methods; and the historical record of the evidence that was in fact appealed to by protagonists of the rival theories will often provide clues to the domains of evidence that may be appealed to in testing methods against those conflicts.

Two examples should make clear the kind of justification that is envisaged. Consider again the injunction to distrust assignments of functions to parts of the brain if those assignments are based solely on correlations between lesion and behavioural impairment. The history of attempts to localize cerebral functions yields abundant confirmation for this criterion. For of the host of hypotheses about the locations of cerebral functions that have been inspired by such correlations, almost all are entirely without foundation from the standpoint of our present understanding of the brain.[11] Or consider the rule that, other things being equal, biological theories are to be preferred if they are of a kind that holds promise of direct reducibility to physics. Unlike our first example, this is a criterion that is applicable to very substantial theoretical conflicts. By an appeal to the history of biology it could be argued with some plausibility that the criterion is misguided. The argument would appeal, for example, to the sterility, from the standpoint of current physiological theory, of the German biophysical school of physiology in the latter half of the nineteenth century compared with the fertility of physiological researches in the same period that concentrated on the links between organic functions and chemistry.[12]

To forestall possible misunderstanding it is as well to contrast briefly the proposed appeal to the history of science in testing the reliability of methods of theory assessment to certain other proposed justificatory uses of history.

Imre Lakatos famously held that the history of science provides the testing-ground for methodologies.[13] Many difficulties arise in exegesis of Lakatos's views, and an extensive secondary literature

[11] See, for example, the examples cited in W. Bechtel, 'Two common errors in explaining biological and psychological phenomena', *Philosophy of Science*, 49 (1982), 549–74, pp. 551–6.

[12] On nineteenth-century German biophysics see K. E. Rothschuh, 'Ursprünge und Wandlungen der physiologischen Denkweisen im 19. Jahrhundert', in W. Treue and K. Mauel, eds., *Naturwissenschaft, Technik und Wirtschaft im 19. Jahrhundert*, vol. 1, Göttingen, 1976, 135–59, and C. A. Culotta, 'German biophysics, objective knowledge and romanticism', *Historical Studies in the Physical Sciences*, 4 (1974), 3–38.

[13] I have found useful the interpretation of Lakatos's views on justification of methodology given by S. Wykstra, 'The Interdependence of History of Science and Philosophy of Science: Toward a Meta-Theory of Scientific Rationality', unpublished Ph.D. thesis, University of Pittsburgh, 1978, and J. A. Kourany, 'Towards an empirically adequate theory of science', *Philosophy of Science*, 49 (1982), 526–48.

has blossomed. The following contrasts between Lakatosian use of history and that sketched above are, however, gross enough to be insensitive to most of the hotly contended niceties of interpretation. First, their aims differ greatly. Lakatos is concerned to justify a general and, in principle, universally applicable methodology—his methodology of research programmes—against other general methodologies: inductivism, conventionalism, naïve falsification-ism, etc. Our concern, on the other hand, is with the piecemeal justification of particular, often only locally applicable and often theoretical context-sensitive, methods for the assessment of theories. Further, Lakatos's concern is not with the reliabilities of different methodologies, but with their capacities to make sense of the history of science as the product of rational inquiry. There is considerable ambiguity in Lakatos's writings on the way in which a methodology may be shown to make rational sense of the history of science. Sometimes he seems to suggest that what matters is simply the sheer amount of the history of science that can be shown to have been rational according to the standards set by a methodology; but elsewhere the emphasis is on the capacities of methodologies to explicate certain past theory changes that are 'obviously progress-ive', at least as viewed by the scientific élite.[14] This latter emphasis may make Lakatos's appeal to the history of science appear similar to that endorsed here; but such an appearance is dispelled once it is observed that the obviously progressive developments in the history of science are, for Lakatos, the ones in which it was obviously rational to opt for the successor theory: progress and rationality are rarely linked by Lakatos with approximation to the truth or increase in truth content.[15] A third major difference between our approach and the Lakatosian one follows immediately from the difference in aims just noted. The Lakatosian approach ties the adequacy of a methodology to its capacity to represent the types of reasons that

[14] The former criterion is to the fore in 'Falsification and the methodology of research programmes', in I. Lakatos and A. Musgrave, eds., *Criticism and the Growth of Knowledge*, Cambridge, 1970, 91–196. The latter is in evidence in 'History of science and its rational reconstructions', in R. C. Buck and R. S. Cohen, eds., *Boston Studies in the Philosophy of Science*, vol. 8, Dordrecht, 1971, 91–135; capacity to explicate the rationality of paradigmatically rational theory choices is similarly proposed as a test of methodologies by L. Laudan, *Progress and its Problems*, Berkeley, 1977, 155–63.
[15] Lakatos's unconcern with truth as a basis for the objectivity of science is emphasized by I. Hacking, 'Imre Lakatos' philosophy of science', *British Journal for the Philosophy of Science*, 30 (1978), 381–410.

were in fact efficacious in bringing about resolutions of theoretical conflicts.[16] The approach proposed here is solely concerned with the capacity of the methods under test to yield what are, from the standpoint of current scientific consensus, the correct resolutions of past theoretical conflicts. As noted above, the historical record of reasons that were in fact appealed to in justification of past theories may be of great heuristic value in the quest for standard conflicts by which to test the reliability of a particular method. Moreover, as we shall see in Chapter IX, gross discrepancies between the criteria that were in fact effective in resolving theoretical conflicts and the criteria to which we would appeal if faced with those same conflicts would pose a threat to scientific absolutism. But despite their interest in these other respects, past reasons play no essential role in the method of calibration proposed here.

A variety of modes of a posteriori justification of scientific methods has figured in this chapter. We have discussed ways in which reliability may be established by calibration against standards both in connection with measurement and perceptual methods and in connection with methods for the assessment of theories. It has been argued that the quest for such 'surface' justifications of scientific methods constitutes a routine part of scientific inquiry. As well as such routine calibrations we have outlined the way in which the history of science may be exploited as a source of standards against which to test the reliabilities of methods of theory assessment. Where calibration purports only to show that methods are reliable, theoretical analysis of instruments and perceptual mechanisms may yield a deeper type of justification, not only showing methods to be reliable, but also explaining that reliability. The question of the viability of a programme that would provide analogous 'deep' justifications for methods of theory assessment has been touched on, and is further explored in the next chapter. We conclude this chapter by briefly contrasting the types of a posteriori justifications mooted above to certain other approaches, which promise to naturalize epistemology by appeal to psychology and evolutionary theory.

[16] Both Lakatos's talk of the 'reconstruction' of the history of science and his openly cavalier attitude to the scholarly fine structure of history might be taken to imply a lack of concern with reasons actually operative in the past; but his repeated claims that an adequate methodology can explain aspects of scientific development gainsay this (cf. Kourany's convincing 'rational reconstruction' of Lakatos's use of history, 'Towards an empirically adequate theory of science', 537–41).

In the philosophical, psychological, and physiological writings of Hermann von Helmholtz, the grandfather of naturalized epistemology, a recurrent theme is that of the ways in which perceptual psychology and physiology promise to elucidate the circumstances under which the deliverances of the senses are to be trusted. In addition to this, Helmholtz offered extensive speculations on the ways in which perceptual beliefs may arise through processes of interpretation and reinterpretation of sensory cues.[17] Helmholtz's claim that the formation of perceptual beliefs is mediated by 'unconscious' inferential processes analogous to those involved in the formulation and assessment of scientific hypotheses has inspired an extraordinary range of epistemological speculations.

It has been widely thought that study of the modes of formation of our perceptual beliefs, and of our passively acquired general beliefs about the world and our situation in it may yield results that have implications for normative epistemology. The supposition that discovery of the natures of innate cognitive processes would have such implications is commonly backed up by the argument that a measure of reliability is guaranteed by their having originated through processes of natural selection. This kind of programme for a naturalized epistemology is subject to well-known, if inconclusive, objections. Von Helmholtz supposed only that analogies between processes of hypothesis formulation and testing and processes of formation of perceptual beliefs may be of heuristic value in psychological research. It is a far cry from this to the assumption that we are armed with innate procedures for hypothesis formation and assessment, an assumption that is needed if this sort of naturalized epistemology is to get off the ground. Even if the assumption is granted, the argument from natural selection for the reliability of such procedures is of dubious efficacy. Of course, it must be conceded that grossly unreliable innate procedures would have been eliminated by natural selection. But if this programme is to contribute in a serious way to normative epistemology it surely has to promise more than confirmation of the unreliability of obviously unreliable procedures. Rather, it must hold out the prospect of adjudication between procedures that are plausible as

[17] This aspect of Helmholtz's theory of knowledge is interestingly treated in T. C. Meijering, 'Naturalistic Epistemology: Helmholtz and the Rise of a Cognitive Theory of Perception', unpublished Ph.D. thesis, University of California, Berkeley, 1981, ch. 10.

effective guides to scientific inquiry. It seems, however, unlikely that natural selection should have had the power to achieve such accurate discriminations of procedures with respect to their reliabilities; for it is hard to see why, beyond certain thresholds, reliability should be of selective advantage. Worse, it seems that natural selection ought often to have favoured procedures on grounds at odds with reliability—opting, for example, for fast procedures that sometimes mistake lions for wildebeest or yellow rocks as against procedures that diagnose lions more reliably, but so slowly as to let them pounce on the diagnostician. Despite these pessimistic remarks, it should, I think, be admitted that empirical confirmation of the efficacy of this type of naturalized epistemology is on the cards. Perhaps, after all, there are substantive genetically programmed methods for the assessment of hypotheses and perhaps survival potential is more sensitive to their reliability than one might suppose.

The question of empirical plausibility becomes yet more pressing in the case of so-called 'genetic epistemologies', in which the stages by which the child's world-picture is built up are matched with stages in the historical elaboration of a scientific world-picture. An adequate discussion of the various brands of genetic epistemology would take us far afield. But it should be noted that belief in the existence of substantial similarities between the cognitive develop-ment of 'the child' and the cognitive development of 'the human race' has been based on very varied theoretical assumptions. In Herbert Spencer's work, for example, the view that individual cognitive development recapitulates the cognitive development of the race rests upon a belief in the heritability of acquired mental capacities, a belief that would nowadays be described as Lamarck-ian.[18] In the writings of Jean Piaget, however, the underlying assumption appears to be that cognitive development in the two domains is governed by common laws of transformation, in accordance with which corresponding structures of thought emerge in corresponding sequences.[19]

[18] For Spencer's naturalistic epistemology see M. Mandelbaum, *History, Man and Reason*, Baltimore, 1972, 298–304; and C. U. M. Smith, 'Herbert Spencer's epigenetic epistemology', *Studies in History and Philosophy of Science*, 14 (1983), 1–22.

[19] It should be emphasized that this is a minor strand in Piaget's genetic epistemology: the primary relevance of developmental psychology to epistemology claimed by Piaget and his followers concerns its capacity to call in question certain alleged empirical presuppositions of traditional epistemologies.

The genetic epistemology of Piaget and his followers is on the face of it very different from the evolutionary epistemology associated with the names of Toulmin, Popper, and Donald Campbell.[20] Here the methods that have mediated scientific progress are supposedly illuminated not by developmental psychology, but by the fundamental processes of organic evolution: 'blind' variation and selection. But there is a notable similarity between the two epistemological programmes. Like the Piagetian epistemologist the evolutionary epistemologist sees the same developmental processes at work in different domains, despite the lack of any evident causal link that would serve to explain the parallelism.

The analogies drawn by evolutionary epistemologists between the genesis and selection of fortuitous mutations and the genesis and selection of theories have been widely criticized;[21] and Piaget's analogies between the cognitive development of the child and the processes that have mediated scientific progress, whilst much more appealing, are so vague as to offer the critic little purchase. Further, there are grave difficulties both of credibility and of comprehensibility in the claim that developmental processes in such causally disjoined domains might be subject to common laws. It is, perhaps, well for the doctrines defended in this work that genetic and evolutionary epistemology are not robust contenders for our allegiance; for the thought that we are the locus of methods and cognitive structures that develop in accordance with their own intrinsic laws, far from reinforcing the hope that there is no limit to our capacity to achieve reliable resolutions of general questions, is apt to inspire the fear that there may be limits to our knowledge that we cannot by virtue of our cognitive constitution overcome.

---

[20] S. Toulmin, *Human Understanding*, Oxford, 1972; K. Popper, *Objective Knowledge*, London, 1972; D. T. Campbell, 'Evolutionary epistemology', in P. Schilpp, ed., *The Philosophy of Karl Popper*, La Salle, Illinois, 1974, 413–63.

[21] Variously damaging criticisms of evolutionary epistemology are to be found in J. Losee, 'Limitations of an evolutionist philosophy of science', *Studies in History and Philosophy of Science*, 8 (1977), 349–52; P. Skagestad, 'Taking evolution seriously: critical comments on D. T. Campbell's Evolutionary Epistemology', *The Monist*, 61 (1978), 611–21; P. Thagard, 'Against evolutionary epistemology', in P. D. Asquith and R. N. Giere, eds., *PSA 1980*, vol. 1, E. Lansing, Michigan, 1980, 187–96; and C. J. Hookway, 'Naturalism, fallibilism, evolutionary epistemology', in C. J. Hookway, ed., *Mind, Machines and Evolution*, Cambridge, 1984.

VIII

Reliability and Inquiry 2: World-Tracking

In the last chapter we were concerned with ways in which the reliabilities of scientific methods and criteria may be established by calibration against precedents and standards. Mention was made of a more ambitious approach to the justification of methods of theory assessment, one that would seek not only to exhibit their reliability, but also to provide scientific explanations for that reliability. This programme promises to explain the reliabilities of methods by showing how their use constitutes inquirers as sensitive detectors of theoretical states of affairs, as 'world-trackers' to adopt Robert Nozick's memorable metaphor.[1] Such explanations would invoke causal processes originating in states of affairs, eventuating in consensual beliefs, and mediated by states of the sense organs and brains of inquirers; and those causal processes would be so specified as to show the contents of the eventual beliefs to be reliably diagnostic for the initial states of affairs.

From the standpoint of a realist account of truth causal explicability of the reliability of scientific methods of the kind promised by the world-tracking programme is not merely an agreeable possibility. Suppose truth in science is envisaged as representation of a mind-independent real world. It will then appear miraculous should any scientific method be reliably productive of truth unless there is a causal explanation of that reliability, an explanation that shows how it comes about that users of the method are reliable detectors of the way the world is. So on pain of making the attainment of scientific knowledge through methodical inquiry a miracle, causal explicability of the reliability of scientific methods must be postulated.

From the pragmatic standpoint of the present work the feasibility

---

[1] R. Nozick, *Philosophical Explanations*, Oxford, 1981, 178 ff. A sketch of a world-tracking programme is to be found in B. A. O. Williams, *Ethics and the Limits of Philosophy*, London, 1985, ch. 8. Elements of such a programme are adumbrated in much recent writing on 'externalist' or 'reliabilist' conceptions of justification: see, e.g., A. I. Goldman, 'What is justified belief?', in G. Pappas, ed., *Justification and Knowledge. New Studies in Epistemology*, Dordrecht, 1979, 1–23; F. F. Schmitt, 'Justification as reliable indicator or reliable process', *Philosophical Studies*, 40 (1981), 409–17.

of the world-tracking programme does not have the same urgency that it has from the metaphysical realist standpoint. The programme is, however, exciting on several scores. To start with it holds out the prospect of a substantial reinforcement of the case for scientific absolutism against the threat posed by underdetermination of theory. For we may reasonably expect that such understanding of the mechanisms which underlie the reliability of methods of scientific inquiry would result in a great extension in range and sophistication of methods whose reliability could be well established. Further, the programme aims at explanations that are realist in the sense that they account for the genesis of belief through causal processes that originate in 'the outside world'. We have here a notable addition to the already large stock of realist theses that can be accommodated despite our rejection of the metaphysical realist view of truth as correspondence to a mind-independent world. Finally, the vision of the growth of scientific knowledge that the programme would substantiate is immensely attractive in its own right, reconciling as it would a fully naturalistic explanation of scientific progress with a view of progress as achieved by methodical and critical pursuit of scientific knowledge.[2]

For all its manifold attractions the world-tracking programme faces a host of problems. To start with, it is unclear how the immensely complex processes that may lead to scientific consensus are to be categorized for purposes of analysis in accordance with the programme. Would it be useful to maintain a distinction between contexts of discovery and contexts of justification? Or would some more elaborate breakdown be more profitable, for example Goldman's generation-pursuit-test-decision scheme or Cohen's generation-commitment-dissemination-acceptance scheme?[3] The level at which causal explanations of the required sort are to be sought is

---

[2] A further attraction of the world-tracking programme may arise in the context of accounts of propositional knowledge. If justification of belief is analysed in terms of formation and maintenance by reliable methods, the world-tracking programme may be used to link questions about justification of scientific beliefs with questions about their causal ancestry. It thus ties together issues of justification, reliability, and causal ancestry in a way that may perhaps resolve some of the issues between justificationist, causal, and reliabilist accounts of knowledge. In this connection the 'reliable process' account of propositional knowledge proposed by F. F. Schmitt is of particular interest: 'Knowledge, justification and reliability', *Synthese*, 55 (1983), 209–29.

[3] A. I. Goldman, 'Epistemology and the theory of problem solving', *Synthese*, 55 (1983), 21–48; I. B. Cohen, *Revolution in Science*, Cambridge, Mass., 1985, ch. 2.

yet more unclear. Will the explanations be primarily individualistic, concerned with the neurophysiological and psychological processes whereby particular inquirers are constituted as world-trackers? Will they rather be holistic in form, the paradigmatic world-trackers being social entities—communities of inquirers, scientific organizations, disciplines, etc.? Or will the social psychodynamics of the future render this distinction between levels of explanation obsolete?

A different line of objection arises on the score of circularity. As noted in the last chapter, an a posteriori case for the reliability of a method M must, on pain of circularity, satisfy certain conditions. The case should not depend upon premises whose warrant is seriously called in question when the reliability of M is called in question. Further, the argument for the reliability of M should not involve an application of M itself. These constraints impose definite limitations on the pay-off that can be expected of any programme for the naturalization of epistemology. In particular, justification of a complete scientific methodology is ruled out. In the case of surface justification of scientific methods, these constraints leave ample room for a strategy of piecemeal checking of the reliabilities of particular methods carried out against the background of extensive bodies of science and scientific method that are not thereby called in question. In the case of the deep explanatory justifications promised by the world-tracking programme, however, the issue of circularity remains problematic even when the explanations are, hypothetically, delivered piecemeal rather than at a stroke for whole methodologies. For it is to be presumed that all such explanations would draw on substantial portions of theoretical knowledge from a variety of disciplines—physics, chemistry, neurophysiology, psychology, sociology, etc. It is hard to see how in practice one might resolve the question of the indispensability of the method under consideration for the warrant of the premises of the explanation, when those premises comprise a considerable and diverse body of science. Indeed, there is room for the suspicion that questions of the form, 'Is M indispensable for the warrant of T?', where T is a substantial and diverse body of theory, may often be ill posed.

It is, however, a third line of objection that seems to me to pose the gravest threat to the world-tracking programme, at least in its more ambitious forms.

To set out this objection a little preliminary terminology is needed. Let *M* be a method or procedure and the belief that *p* a possible outcome of its employment. We say that *M* is diagnostic for state of affairs *p* in range *R* just in case when use of *M* yields the belief that *p*, its so doing is a reliable indicator that if any state in *R* holds that state is *p*.[4] If the range *R* exhausts the logical possibilities, *M* is a *decision procedure* for *p*. If *R* is not exhaustive of the logical possibilities, *M* is a *choice procedure* for *p*. When *M* is diagnostic for all states in range *R* we say that *M* is *discriminant* in *R*.

The world-tracking programme requires that we specify and explain the reliabilities of procedures diagnostic for both observable and theoretical states of affairs. At the perceptual end of the spectrum of methods we might have, for example, methods for judging under appropriate circumstances the directions of the sources of sounds, the relative distances of objects, or the reflectances of surfaces. At a somewhat more theoretical level we might have, for instance, methods for identifying chemical substances or biological species. Yet further up the theoretical scale one may envisage, say, methods for determining the spins of fundamental particles or for establishing the molecular mechanisms of postsynaptic inhibition. And at the theoretical extreme one may dream of such wonders as methods for ascertaining how many fundamental forces there are, or what the affine structure of space-time is. (In passing it should be noted that these are all instances of discriminant methods. The argument which follows applies equally to diagnostic methods that are not discriminant in their ranges, for example methods for detecting concert pitch but not other pitches, or for recognizing Great Crested Grebes but not other species of grebes.)

At the perceptual end of the scale the prospects for explaining the reliabilities of diagnostic methods seem good indeed. Of course, we are far from having a complete account of the mechanisms that underlie even the most straightforward methods of formation of perceptual judgements. Nor should it be forgotten that even at this level explanations of the reliable achievement of scientific consensus would have to concern themselves not only with the formation of perceptual judgements, but also, and perhaps much more problematically, with the processes of social negotiation that may

---

[4] There are many intractable difficulties in spelling out what it is for a method to yield, or be responsible for, a belief: see, e.g., R. Nozick, *Philosophical Explanations*, Oxford, 1981, 179 ff.

eventuate in the certification of perceptual judgements as scientific data. Nevertheless, the current state of research in psychology and neurophysiology of perception does allow the formation of hypotheses about causal processes that eventuate via events in the sense organs in psychological states that are under appropriate circumstances reliably discriminant of, for example, pitches, reflectances of surfaces, relative distances, etc.[5] At the perceptual end of the scale, then, we have to hand some at least of the materials that might be needed for explanation of the reliability of a diagnostic method in accordance with the world-tracking programme.

As we move towards the theoretical end of the spectrum it becomes progressively harder to escape a sense of unreality in the world-tracking programme. Partly this may arise from the ever-increasing magnitudes of the blank cheques drawn on the future sciences that are to provide explanations of the reliabilities of methods diagnostic for theoretical states of affairs. But there is, I think, a further reason for unease about extrapolation of the programme from the perceptual into the theoretical domain: namely, that it is hard to see how methods diagnostic for highly theoretical states of affairs are to be formulated.

As noted above, diagnostic methods divide into decision procedures, when the range of states of affairs over which they are diagnostic is exhaustive, and choice procedures, when it is not. Decision procedures for all kinds of states of affairs are readily formulated. If p is a state of affairs, we simply take as our range p and *not-p*. This is not a helpful move. As is generally agreed, the prospects for discovery of reliable decision procedures for highly theoretical states of affairs are dim indeed. Choice procedures look rather more promising; but then the question arises as to how the non-exhaustive ranges on which they are defined are to be specified. When we consider observable and low-level theoretical states of affairs, the specification of plausible ranges for choice procedures is unproblematic. We have, for example, methods for telling, given that an organism is a butterfly of a type 'known to science', to which species it belongs, or, given that a substance is a polypeptide in a pure state, what its molecular weight is. As we move towards the theoretical end of the spectrum of states of affairs, however, it

---

[5] My impression of the current state of perceptual psychology is based on a reading of papers in H. B. Barlow and J. D. Mollon, eds., *The Senses*, Cambridge, 1984.

becomes progressively harder to envisage ranges over which diagnostic methods might operate. What could constitute an appropriate range of alternative hypotheses about, say, the affine structure of space-time or the number of fundamental forces in the universe?

On certain accounts of propositional knowledge it is allowed that *p* may be known even when it is not known that *not-p*, provided that each of some non-exhaustive range of relevant contrary alternatives to *p* is known not to obtain. Consideration of some of the suggestions that have been made in this context may prove instructive in our present quandary.[6] Here are some sufficient conditions that have been suggested for a state of affairs *q* to be a relevant contrary alternative to a state of affairs *p*, in the sense that it must be known not to obtain if *p* is to be known to obtain.

1. *q* is a relevant contrary alternative if it is sufficiently probable.

2. *q* is a relevant contrary alternative if the nearest *q*-world is sufficiently close to the actual world.

3. *q* is a relevant contrary alternative if there are data that would sufficiently justify the belief that *q*.

4. *q* is a relevant contrary alternative if there is a belief-forming process that would sufficiently justify the belief that *q*.

Of these conditions it is the first that seems the most germane to our concern with reliable methods. Like the other conditions it is strongly theory dependent, at least when applied to theoretical states of affairs, in the sense that it is only in the context of background theories that one could use it to determine a range. It is, I think, such theory dependence that is responsible for the difficulty in specification of ranges for diagnostic methods in the case of highly theoretical states of affairs. When low-level theoretical states of affairs are at issue there will generally be a substantial theoretical background, neutral with respect to the alternatives at issue, that can be appealed to in determining which states of affairs are the more probable. When, however, highly theoretical states are at issue, there will often be little such neutral background, so that

---

6 On cognitively relevant contrary alternatives see, e.g., P. Yourgrau, 'Knowledge and relevant alternatives', *Synthese*, 55 (1983), 175–90; R. K. Shope, *The Analysis of Knowing. A Decade of Research*, Princeton, 1983, 158 ff., 223 ff.; Schmitt, 'Knowledge, justification and reliability', 211–13.

determination of a range of relatively probable states becomes highly problematic.

In Chapter VI we discussed difficulties for the resolution of major theoretical conflicts that arise from theory-loading of the notion of evidence. The present difficulty is in certain respects similar, and it may be that it can be resolved along similar lines, by arguing that despite appearances there will always in fact be a sufficient body of neutral background theory. However, a discouraging difference between the cases should be noted. In the case of theoretical conflict the quest is generally for background theories that are neutral with respect to non-exhaustive pairs of alternative solutions to theoretical questions. In the present case, however, our concern is with the selection from total ranges of possible alternative theoretical states of affairs of those that are most probable. The quest is therefore for background theories that are neutral with respect to exhaustive ranges of solutions to theoretical questions. Such neutrality is a tall order.

Despite the difficulties faced by the world-tracking programme it is my hunch that deep justifications of methods of theory assessment will one day be forthcoming. These are serious difficulties, however; and though the world-tracking programme is surely not the only possible programme for deep justification, it is a salient one. In conclusion it is worth considering in a little more detail the consequences should failure be the fate of all projects of deep justification of scientific methods through causal explanation of their reliability.

Suppose that there are scientific methods that have ample surface justification by calibration against standards and precedents, but for which there is no hope of deep justification. As already intimated, reflection on this possibility brings out a major difference between the realist metaphysical standpoint and the pragmatic standpoint of this work. From the realist standpoint reliability of a scientific method is miraculous if that reliability is causally inexplicable. However well attested by calibration the reliability of a method may be, the realist had better not concede its reliability if it does not admit of deep justification. And should the reliability of methods that have played substantial roles in the development of science prove unamenable to deep justification, a case for scepticism about the accumulation of truth in science emerges. From the realist standpoint scientific absolutism and causal explanation of the reliability of scientific methods are intimately linked: the former presupposes the possibility of the latter.

From our pragmatic standpoint the position is quite different. Success of programmes for deep justification of scientific methods may one day strengthen the case for scientific absolutism. But the failure of such programmes is not a serious threat to it. It does not menace it directly; for from the pragmatic standpoint there are no grounds for holding that causal inexplicability of the reliability of a scientific method renders its reliability miraculous. Nor does it menace it indirectly by implying insuperable limitations on our capacity to answer a particular type of theoretical question; for we have no antecedent grounds for holding the demand for specification of causal mechanisms underlying the reliability of methods to be a legitimate demand.

Should surface justification of scientific methods—establishment of their reliabilities by calibration against precedents and standards—fail, then scientific absolutism is surely doomed. Should deep justification of scientific methods—that is, causal explanation of their reliability—fail, then there are ample grounds for disappointment, but collapse of scientific absolutism is not one of them.

IX

Limits of Inquiry

PERHAPS the most vulnerable of the hypotheses about the fortunes of an indefinitely prolonged human inquiry on which our defence of scientific absolutism rests is the claim that such an inquiry would show an unlimited capacity to achieve reliable resolutions of general questions. We have already defended the infinite resolution hypothesis at length against arguments for the underdetermination of theory by data. In the course of that defence it was conceded that certain 'internal' cosmological questions may well be irresoluble by us by virtue of our situation in the universe. In this chapter we shall reflect further on this and a variety of other pressing cases for the irresolubility of specific types of general questions.

Some preliminary pre-emptive remarks are in order. First, it should be noted that to challenge the infinite resolution hypothesis it does not suffice to make out a case for the unattainability of complete theoretical understanding in a domain of inquiry. Thus, to take an example mentioned earlier, Emil Du Bois-Reymond's claim that science will never comprehend the conditions for the emergence of life does not constitute a challenge if interpreted as maintaining only that, no matter how prolonged our inquiries, we would never be able to give a complete account of the origin of life. To constitute an effective challenge a case must be made for supposing that there are specific general questions about the origin of life—Does it require a carbon-based chemistry? Is polymerization of macromolecules on crystal surfaces an essential stage? etc— that would forever prove irresoluble. Though obvious, this is an important point. As urged in Chapter II, the history of science militates against the idea that our scientific inquiries are convergent on an ultimate theory or collection of theories; so commitment to the eventual attainability of complete understanding in each of the domains of scientific inquiry would be fatal to the case for scientific absolutism.

A second pre-emptive remark concerns the resolution of questions of the forms 'What is the explanation of . . .?' and 'How is . . .

to be explained?' Without defending my position, since to do so would involve engagement in controversial issues concerning the nature of explanation, I shall take it that when events can be shown to be causally undetermined the need for further explanation is removed. I shall also assume that there may be scientific hypotheses that require no explanation. The assumptions are crucial ones for the defence of the thesis of infinite resolution of general questions: for in the absence of the first the thesis is threatened by the indeterministic claims of our best physical theories; and in the absence of the second it is false should there exist fundamental laws.

Finally, and most importantly, it should be reiterated that the infinite resolution hypothesis does not require that each outstanding general question be determinable given sufficiently prolonged inquiry. Rather, it is required that each outstanding general question be either determinable or dissoluble given sufficiently prolonged inquiry. Some of the many strategies for the dissolution of questions were touched on in Chapters III and IV. Perhaps the most straightforward strategy, and the one most apt to deliver clear-cut results, is that of seeking to dissolve a question by showing it to have a false presupposition. Other strategies seek to reveal questions as ill posed by showing them to be entirely unamenable to all evidential considerations. One such strategy seeks to impugn the totality of the evidence that may be called upon to resolve a question. (Along these lines, for example, it might be claimed that questions in psychoanalytical theory that are entirely dependent for their determination on the interpretation of dreams are ill posed because the supposed evidence is illegitimate, being irreplicable.) Alternatively, the target may be the methods that have to be employed if evidence is to be brought to bear on a question. (Along these lines one might mount a further attack on the well-posedness of questions in psychoanalytic theory which depend for their determination on methods of dream interpretation, arguing that all such methods are illegitimate. I hasten to add that I do not endorse these particular examples.) A proper treatment of the various modes of dissolution of questions would be a large undertaking. For our purposes, however, it suffices to note the historical prevalence of dissolution of questions once thought to be deep and intractable.

With these provisos in mind let us survey some putative specific limits to human inquiry.

It has already been conceded that our current general physical theory may, in combination with plausible cosmological models, imply the insolubility of certain cosmological questions. Should cosmological models of this sort be well confirmed, the case for limits to human inquiry would be peculiarly compelling. For the case for unanswerability rests on the inaccessibility of particular types of evidence that would definitely resolve the cosmological questions at issue. The very argument for unanswerability of such a question therefore provides grounds for supposing it to be well posed.

A second category of claims about limits to human inquiry concerns limits which are discernible through philosophical reflection rather than becoming manifest in the course of scientific inquiry. Such are claims about the irresolubility of certain explanatory questions that appear to transcend scientific inquiry by virtue of their generality: Why is there something rather than nothing? Why is the cosmos to some extent law-governed rather than entirely chaotic? etc.[1] To this category belong claims about the irresolubility of questions concerning the grounds of consciousness and the freedom of the will. Here too belongs the claim that limits on the capacity of science to understand the conditions for its own emergence can be established a priori, for example, by showing that were those limits transcended scientists would have *per impossibile* the capacity to predict the contents of future science.[2]

A third category of hypothetical limits includes those that we may encounter not within our own inquiries, whether scientific or philosophical, but rather through an encounter with systems of belief that are temporally, culturally, or biologically far removed from our own. We have already touched on and sought to discount the possibility of two such types of encounters: encounters with beings possessed of a science transcending our own, but whose beliefs remain, come what may, inscrutable by us; and encounters with alien belief systems that are in global or near global conflict with our own. Our concern here will be with ways in which a more parochial kind of encounters, namely encounters with past systems of scientific beliefs and practices, may suggest the existence of limits to our capacity to resolve general questions.

Systematic study of the history of scientific methodology is an

---

[1] Cf. N. Rescher, *The Limits of Science*, Berkeley, 1984, 118 ff.
[2] Cf. K. R. Popper, *The Poverty of Historicism*, London, 1957, preface.

enterprise of fairly recent origin. However, there is compelling prima facie evidence for a great diversity of styles of scientific inquiry in different periods and disciplines. To cite a few striking examples: Hacking has made out a case for denying the existence prior to the seventeenth century of anything at all close to current conceptions of inductive support for theories by empirical evidence;[3] Foucault and others have documented the displacement in the course of the seventeenth century of modes of analogical reasoning associated with the doctrines of man as microcosm and of the universe as a text to be deciphered;[4] and Laudan has made out a solid case for the prevalence of hypothetico-deductive methodology in seventeenth-century corpuscular-mechanical science followed by a period of abeyance until the nineteenth-century revival of hypothetico-deductivism.[5]

The 'case from serendipity' for the existence of limits to human inquiry arises whenever there are gross discrepancies between, on the one hand, the methods whose application was in fact effective in yielding what were, from the standpoint of our theories, correct resolutions of theoretical conflicts and, on the other hand, methods that are, by our lights, reliable—the ones to which we would appeal to resolve those same conflicts. Should such situations frequently arise, the history of science would manifest progress by luck— serendipity.[6] A serious challenge would be posed to our capacity to explain the growth of scientific knowledge as the product of reliable methods of inquiry. Evidence for the diversity of styles of scientific inquiry, however, makes it seem likely that such situations are widely prevalent.

The 'case from well-posedness' kicks off from the apparently uncontentious claim that the range of questions that are well posed for members of a community of inquirers, the range of questions that are 'real' for them, is not fixed but rather dependent on the language, beliefs, cognitive capacities, and situation in the universe of members of that community. Let us call whatever it is that

[3] I. Hacking, *The Emergence of Probability*, Cambridge, 1975.

[4] M. Foucault, *Les mots et les choses*, Paris, 1966, chs. 2 and 3.

[5] L. Laudan, *Science and Hypothesis*, Dordrecht, 1981. Much further evidence of diversity of styles of inquiry is to be found in A. C. Crombie's major forthcoming work *Styles of Scientific Thinking in the European Tradition*.

[6] Horace Walpole derived 'serendipity' from the title of a fairy tale, *The Princes of Serendip*, whose heroes 'were always making discoveries by accidents and sagacity'.

determines the domain of questions well posed for members of a community of inquirers 'the categorial framework' of that community. There is considerable diversity of views on the nature of categorial frameworks. Some accounts would assign but a single categorial framework to all mankind, whilst admitting the possibility of alien inquirers with different frameworks. Such are 'biologized' Kantian accounts, which treat the range of questions well posed for us as conditioned by our perceptual and cognitive faculties. Of more immediate concern are accounts which imply differences of categorial framework between communities of human inquirers. Thus it may be claimed that the semantics of the language of a community determines the range of questions well-posed for its members.[7] Again, it may be claimed that it is the total body of knowledge they possess that determines the range of questions well posed for inquirers.[8] Alternatively, it may be claimed that the range of questions well posed for the members of a community is determined by their disciplinary practices and regimes.[9] Or, in a related vein, it may be claimed that the range of questions well posed for members of a community is determined by their style of inquiry, a question being well posed for them only if their style of inquiry is one that is able, at least in principle, to 'get to grips' with it.[10]

If there has in fact been a diversity of styles of scientific inquiry, then the last of these conditions for well-posedness implies that some questions that are well posed for one community of scientific inquirers will not constitute 'real questions' for other communities of inquirers. The challenge surfaces once we ask how we may justify the 'reality' of the questions well posed from the standpoint of our own style of scientific inquiry in the face of styles of inquiry that determine different ranges of well-posedness. The obvious answer is that to do so we must show our own style of scientific inquiry to be, in so far as it differs from the other styles of inquiry, more reliable than they. On pain of circularity we cannot, in seeking to show our

[7] See, for example, K. Ajdukiewicz, 'Das Weltbild und die Begriffsapparatur', *Erkenntnis*, 4 (1934), 259–87, trans. by J. Wilkinson in J. Giedymin, ed., *Kazimierz Ajdukiewicz: the Scientific World-Perspective and Other Essays, 1931–63*, Dordrecht, 1978, 67–89.

[8] Cf. Rescher, *The Limits of Science*, chs. 2 and 3.

[9] A view promoted, for example, in Michel Foucault's later works.

[10] Cf. I. Hacking, 'Language, truth and reason', in M. Hollis and S. Lukes, eds., *Rationality and Relativism*, Oxford, 1982, 48–66.

own style of inquiry to be more reliable than an alternative style of inquiry, invoke its capacity to answer questions whose well-posedness is called in question by that alternative.[11] In case the styles of inquiry have little in common there may, it seems, be no 'neutral ground' on which an unbiased assessment of reliability can be conducted.[12] Should the conclusion have to be conceded, then we shall have to admit that our capacity to resolve general questions is limited, not because there are well-posed questions that we can never hope to answer, but rather because we cannot hope to tell of a wide range of questions whether or not they are well posed. In Chapter III well-posedness of questions was related to their susceptibility to evidential considerations. Since differences in style of scientific inquiry will be reflected in different conceptions of susceptibility to evidential considerations, we are bound to take this last version of the argument from well-posedness very seriously indeed.

Before examining the credentials of these varied arguments for the existence of limits to human inquiry, let us further explore certain of their consequences.

First let us consider the implications of the irreducible dependence of well-posedness of questions on categorial frameworks. Like other relativist doctrines, this one is incoherent if supposed to be of universal scope, an incoherence that emerges when we ask whether the question, 'Is the well-posedness of questions irreducibly relative to categorial framework?', is well posed absolutely or only relative to some categorial framework. However, the more modest claim that the well-posedness of some questions, perhaps in certain domains of inquiry all questions, is irreducibly relative to categorial framework is surely a coherent one.

Relativism about well-posedness is to be sharply distinguished from relativism about truth, according to which a proposition may have no absolute-truth value whilst taking different relative-truth values from different standpoints or with respect to different categorial frameworks. It has often been argued that relativism

---

[11] Cf. ibid., p. 65.

[12] Hacking does in fact admit the existence of 'boring' propositions whose 'positivity' does not depend upon style of inquiry (ibid., p. 49). As pointed out by W. Newton-Smith these could provide 'neutral ground' for the assessment of reliabilities of styles of inquiry: 'Relativism and the possibility of interpretation', in Hollis and Lukes, eds., *Rationality and Relativism*, 106–22, pp. 121–2.

about truth remains incoherent even when its scope is restricted to avoid self-refutation.[13] In the context of our pragmatic account of truth it is certainly very hard to see how a coherent version could be constructed. We can indeed readily construct relative notions of truth within that account. For example, a notion of truth-for-humans might be constructed by replacing 'inquiry' by 'human inquiry' throughout. But this does not lead to coherent versions of relativism about truth. Rather, propositions that have a variety of relative-truth values, being, say, true-for-humans and false-for-Martians, will be (absolutely) false.

Relativism about truth, however, like the doctrine often thought of as its antithesis, the correspondence account of truth, has long shown resilience in the face of compelling objections on the score of coherence. As with the correspondence account, it seems that refutation is not enough: to extirpate these doctrines auxiliary tactics are needed. Like the correspondence account, relativism about truth is customarily purveyed by means of stock metaphors. Worlds, horizons, standpoints, perspectives, grids, and frames provide the metaphorical currency. Complete devaluation would be a substantial task; but it may be worth mentioning two lines of deconstructive thought. First, it appears on reflection that certain of these metaphors are suggestive of relativism about well-posedness rather than of relativism about truth. The questions well posed from a standpoint constitute metaphorically a world to be explored: a horizon separates, metaphorically, questions well posed from a standpoint from questions ill posed from that standpoint; and so on. Other relativist metaphors are self-subverting. Like the sustaining metaphors of metaphysical realism they incomprehensibly invoke relations to a transcendent neutral substrate. What is it, after all, that different perspectives project, different schemes organize, and different grids partition?[14]

Arguments for the existence of limits to our capacity to answer well-posed questions have often been taken as conducive to relativism about truth. One such route to relativism is as follows. First, we note that the admission of specific limits to our inquiries may in certain cases induce wide-ranging doubts about our capacity to

[13] See, for example, C. Swoyer, 'True for', in J. W. Meiland and M. Krausz, eds., *Relativism, Cognitive and Moral*, Notre Dame, 1982, 84–108, and W. F. Vallicella, 'Relativism, truth and the symmetry thesis', *The Monist*, 67 (1984), 452–66.

[14] Cf. D. Davidson, 'On the very idea of a conceptual scheme', *Proceedings of the American Philosophical Association*, 47 (1973–4), 5–20.

achieve reliable resolutions of questions. For example, where the initial argument impugns our capacity to answer certain high-level theoretical questions, doubt may spread by a domino effect, 'downwards' to dependent questions in the same field of inquiry, and 'sideways' from that field of inquiry into cognate fields. Where, as with the argument from serendipity already mentioned, the initial doubt concerns our capacity to understand the means whereby we acquire scientific knowledge, the doubt may spread more immediately. For it is a short step from acknowledgement that we cannot explain the genesis of our beliefs in terms of application of reliable methods, to doubt about the validity of those beliefs. The next step, the step to relativism about truth, seeks to evade the case for serious doubt about a wide range of our beliefs by claiming for those beliefs only relative rather than absolute truth, the mode of relativization depending on the type of limit that was alleged at the outset.

Given the incoherence of relativism about truth, it cannot provide the grounds on which to take a stand against scepticism: the sceptical challenges to scientific absolutism must be met case by case by other means. One defensive strategy, the obvious one, is to seek to show that the arguments for existence of specific limits to human inquiry are defective. In the case conceded in Chapter VI, however, that of the probable irresolubility of certain cosmological questions by virtue of inaccessibility of relevant evidence, some other defensive strategy must be found. An alternative strategy attempts to show that a concession of the limit in question does not provide grounds for more general doubt about our capacity to achieve reliable resolution of general questions. If this strategy of mitigation succeeds, then the case for scientific absolutism set out in Chapter IV is readily repaired. There is was argued that the inevitable limitations on our capacity to resolve singular questions do not constitute an ineluctable source of error in our resolution of general questions. From this, in turn, it was argued that the limitations on our capacity to resolve singular questions do not create a discrepancy between truth from the standpoint of an absolute inquiry series and truth from the standpoint of an inquiry series generated by indefinitely protracted human inquiry. In general, if the strategy of mitigation succeeds with respect to some class of questions Q, then the argument of Chapter IV can be adapted to yield the conclusion that our incapacity to resolve questions in Q does not create a gulf between truth from the standpoint of an absolute inquiry series and truth from the standpoint of the products of indefinitely prolonged human inquiry.

Applying the strategy of mitigation to cosmological questions of the type raised by Glymour and Malament, it may be noted that the irresolubility of these questions does not cast doubt on the parts of our physical theory on which the case for their irresolubility itself depends. That is a substantial part, namely the general physical theory which specifies the spatio-temporal limits on accessibility of information by observers at particular spatio-temporal locations. It is tempting to go on to dismiss as fanciful the suggestion that the irresolubility of these questions provides serious grounds for doubt about the reliable resolution of questions in fields other than physics or cosmology. Caution is, however, in order. The history of science is replete with striking examples of the unexpected relevance of questions in one field to questions in far-removed fields; consider, to take a famous instance, the relevance of thermodynamics to theories of organic evolution revealed by Lord Kelvin's calculation of a maximum age for life on earth on the basis of rate of dissipation of solar energy.[15] Once the phenomenon of unexpected interdisciplinary relevance is admitted, the threat of a domino effect is evident. One way of countering this would be to argue by induction on the history of science that even when the answering of specific theoretical questions in one field of inquiry appears indispensable for the reliable resolution of questions in another field, sufficiently prolonged inquiry is very likely to bring to light other relevant theoretical considerations and other sources of evidence. Unfortunately, the conclusion of this line of argument is too ambitious as it stands. For there are surely many high-level theoretical issues whose resolution is genuinely indispensable for the reliable resolution of a range of theoretical issues in cognate fields: think, for example, of the implications for chemistry and biology were fundamental questions in thermodynamics to prove irresoluble. It may, however, be possible to make out a case against the occurrence of such a domino effect when the irresoluble questions are at lower theoretical levels. That would suffice to head off the threat posed by the irresolubility of 'internal' cosmological questions of the types posed by Glymour and Malament.

One who held strong views on the autonomy of the natural

---

[15] See L. Eiseley, *Darwin's Centenary*, Garden City, 1958, ch. 8; J. D. Birchfield, *Lord Kelvin and the Age of the Earth*, New York, 1975.

sciences might well seek to apply the strategy of mitigation to all allegedly irresoluble questions in disciplines beyond the natural scientific pale, arguing that however thoroughly the limits to our inquiries may impugn the attainability of truth in non-scientific disciplines, they cannot induce scepticism within the territory of the natural sciences. The historical evidence, however, for the inextricability of the domains of natural science and metaphysics makes this appear a heroic stance. Further, the obvious and frequent dependence of the resolution of natural scientific questions on the resolution of pure mathematical questions shows the strategy not to be generally applicable.

Before attempting to counter the arguments from well-posedness and serendipity it is worth remarking again that many of the alleged limits to human inquiry appear convincing only if one overlooks the possibility that their eventual resolution may take the form of a demonstration that they are ill posed. Where the supposedly irresoluble question is an explanatory one, it is open to us, as already noted, to seek to resolve it by showing the explanatory demand to be illegitimate. In other cases it is open to us to attempt to dissolve the purportedly unanswerable question by analytical means. For example, it has been argued, in my view convincingly, that our inability to conceive what it is like to be a bat reflects our incapacity to have certain experiences, rather than our incompetence to resolve a well-posed question.[16] Other allegedly insoluble philosophical questions owe their apparent intractability not to the unavailability of considerations germane to their resolution, but rather to the availability of cogent considerations equally balanced pro and con. Here there is room for the hope that the often underrated scholastic device of *distinctio* may break the recalcitrant question down without remainder into questions that are soluble, if not already solved.

Two of the most serious challenges to the infinite resolution thesis, the argument from serendipity and the argument from well-posedness, are premissed on the historical diversity of styles of scientific inquiry. The argument from serendipity arises, it may be remembered, if the following situation has been widespread in the history of science:

(i) conflict between theories T and T' was resolved in favour of T;

---

[16] D. Lewis, 'Postscript to "Mad pain and Martian pain" ', *Philosophical Papers*, vol. 1, Oxford, 1983, 130–2.

(ii) *T* is, from the standpoint of current scientific theories, true or, at least, contains more true components than *T'*;

(iii) the best explanation for the resolution of the conflict in favour of *T* is in terms of application, explicit or tacit, of methods that are by current standards unreliable.

Radical historical diversity of styles of scientific inquiry implies the prevalence of such cases, especially in earlier periods. Similarly, such diversity of styles of inquiry implies the ill-posedness from our standpoint of many of the questions that were, for past inquirers, well posed. As we have seen, this, when taken together with the incommensurability of styles of inquiry with respect to reliability that arises when the divergence of style is substantial, has fatal consequences for the thesis of unlimited resolution of questions by an indefinitely protracted human inquiry.

Earlier the threat to scientific absolutism posed by the alleged occurrence in the history of science of near global confrontations of world-pictures was countered with an attack on the historical premiss. Here too we shall question the historical premiss, asking whether there has in fact been a radical diversity of styles of inquiry in the sense of style of inquiry that is needed to sustain the arguments from serendipity and well-posedness.

The styles of scientific inquiry that relate to the well-posedness of questions and to serendipity in the resolution of theoretical conflicts are constituted by the types of reasoning, deliberation, observation, experiment, etc., through which past consensuses were in fact achieved. Two main sources of evidence about past styles of inquiry may be distinguished. First, there is direct evidence in the form of reasons explicitly offered in confirmation or infirmation of past hypotheses and theories. Secondly, there is the indirect evidence that accrues from past writings about scientific method. Some examples have already been given of evidence of this latter type that appears to show the radical diversity of styles of inquiry. There are, however, a number of reasons for not taking such evidence at face value. To start with many general methodological pronouncements have been at such high levels of abstraction that, even if taken as fair characterizations of scientific practice, they give little genuine indication of the reasons that were in fact effective in resolving theoretical conflicts. Further, there are numerous grounds for doubting whether general methodological pronouncements, even when relatively specific and detailed, provide reliable guides to past scientific practices. In the last chapter it was argued that many of the rules and criteria whose observance is effective in the consensual resolution of scientific conflict are local rules of thumb rather than general precepts. It follows that general methodological pronouncements are suspect simply by virtue of their generality. It was argued, too, that many such rules are tacitly rather than consciously observed. So even the sincerest methodological professions are further suspect, given the unreliability of agents' descriptions of their tacit practices.[17]

When we turn to the direct evidence for past styles of inquiry provided by explicitly presented reasons, the case for substantial diversity remains a strong one. It is, indeed, a commonplace of the history of science that the grounds on which theoretical innovations were promoted and criticized often appear to us alien, irrational, or far-fetched. However, such evidence is potentially misleading. Let us distinguish 'original reasons', the confirmatory reasons offered by the originators and early protagonists of a theory, from 'consensual reasons', the reasons that mediate the consensual adoption of a theory. On occasion the original reasons of a successful theory have much in common with its consensual reasons; but often there are major discrepancies between original and consensual reasons, especially in cases of radical theoretical innovation in which the processes leading to eventual widespread acceptance of the new theory were protracted. The history of science is replete with instances in which the original reasons of a theory appear alien to us, whilst the reasons which led to its eventual establishment are, by our standards, more familiar and sound. Contrast, for example, the numerological and cosmological grounds offered by Rheticus and Kepler in support of Copernican cosmology to the evidence from stellar aberration and parallax that eventually clinched the case for heliocentrism.[18] Or, to take an example nearer home, contrast the

---

[17] Gaston Bachelard is one who often emphasized the discrepancies between scientists' practices and the 'official' methodologies to which they subscribe: see, e.g., *Le materialisme rationel*, Paris, 1953, 20 ff.

[18] For Rheticus' advocacy see his *Narratio prima* (1540), trans. in E. Rosen, *Three Copernican Treatises*, New York, 1939; for Kepler's advocacy see his *Mysterium cosmographicum*, trans. A. M. Duncan, *The Secret of the Universe*, New York, 1981. On the detection of stellar aberration see M. A. Hoskin, 'Hooke, Bradley and the aberration of light', in *Stellar Astronomy*, Chalfont St Giles, 1982, 29–36; on the detection of stellar parallax see, e.g., O. Struve, 'The first stellar parallax determination', in H. M. Evans, ed., *Men and Moments in the History of Science*, Seattle, 1959, 177–206, and M. A. Hoskin, op. cit., 8–11.

relatively inconclusive and sometimes fanciful geomorphological, palaeontological, and palaeoclimatic reasons presented by Wegener and Du Toit in support of the hypothesis of continental drift to the 'hard' evidence from palaeomagmatism and sea-floor spreading that has yielded consensual acceptance in the past decade.[19] This kind of discrepancy between original reasons and the often more familiar and, by our standards, sounder consensual reasons is apt to be obscured by the tendency of many conventional histories of science to concentrate unduly on the opinions of 'great' innovators and prematurely to write off 'loser' theories in favour of 'winners'. The apparent strength of the case for diversity of styles of scientific inquiry is, I suggest, largely a historiographical artefact arising from concern with general methodological pronouncements and original reasons at the expense of consensual reasons.

The argument for the irreducible relativity of the well-posedness of questions to style of scientific inquiry is, as indicated earlier, but one of a family of arguments, all of which pose threats to the thesis of the unlimited resolution of questions. A general form for many arguments for relativism about well-posedness is as follows. Let X be the categorial framework—language, system of disciplines, style of inquiry, cognitive apparatus, etc.—to which the well-posedness of questions is to be shown irreducibly relative. It must be demonstrated:

(i) that the requisite diversity of inquirers with respect to X is possible;

(ii) that well-posedness of questions is dependent on X;

(iii) that there is no way of ranking Xs so as to restore an absolute notion of well-posedness, without a question-begging appeal to the well-posedness of certain questions.

The case in which X = style of inquiry has been countered by challenging the historical evidence used to render (i) plausible. In other instances, where X = language, system of disciplines, or cognitive apparatus, for example, the diversity claim does not appear vulnerable. The cosatisfaction of (ii) and (iii), however, becomes deeply problematic. It is no longer clear, as it is in the case of styles of inquiry, that the well-posedness of questions is dependent on categorial framework; some account of the way in

[19] See A. Hallam, *A Revolution in the Earth Sciences: From Continental Drift to Plate Tectonics*, Oxford, 1973.

which such dependence comes about is needed to render (ii) plausible. But it is hard to see how such an account can be given without at the same time providing a basis on which categorial frameworks may be ranked, and by so doing defeating (iii). Thus an account of the ways in which the well-posedness of questions depends upon language would surely provide the basis for a theory of expressive power of languages, and hence for a ranking of languages with respect to expressive power. Equally, it is hard to envisage an account of the dependence of the well-posedness of questions on ratiocinative or perceptual equipment that would not at the same time provide a basis for escape from relativism though the comparison of cognitive equipments with respect to their powers and reliabilities. In general it is, I suggest, overpreparedness to concede step (ii) in the above scheme that lends credence to relativism about the well-posedness of questions. For to concede this step without insisting on a theoretical account of the way in which biological, linguistic, or social categories determine the well-posedness of questions, is to forswear precisely the means that may provide an escape from relativism. Such overpreparedness is likely to afflict those who hold views in the philosophy of language which tie well-posedness closely to infirmability or confirmability by currently available means; and it is likely also to afflict those who are predisposed to regard our cognitive enterprises as determined by 'blind forces', whether biological, social, or economic. These are, I think, doctrines that can be resisted on grounds unrelated to their conduciveness to relativism; but such resistance lies far beyond the scope of this work.

X

Conclusion: Pragmatic Commitments

OUR defence of scientific absolutism—the claim that the natural sciences have shown an accumulation of truth—is now at an end. The initial hunch was that scientific absolutism is not merely on the surface but through and through a historical thesis. A pragmatic account of truth was set out in the opening chapters of this work and it was argued in the context of that account that scientific absolutism can be inductively confirmed by a complex extrapolation from certain aspects of the history of science. In subsequent chapters scientific absolutism has been defended against the direct threats posed by the thesis of underdetermination of theory by data and by claims about the existence of insuperable limits to human inquiry. It has been defended also against the indirect threats posed by the theses of incommensurability of theories and indeterminacy of intertheoretic interpretation, theses that would undermine the types of interpretation of the history of science on which the historical evidence for scientific absolutism depends.

Let us reflect briefly on some of the epistemological and historiographical commitments that have been incurred in the course of this defence of the truth-amassing nature of science.

Captured 'realist' positions have been proudly paraded in the course of this work. However, the magnitude of the gulf between the pragmatic and realist metaphysical standpoints becomes clear when we contrast our commitments to those incurred by a realist defence of scientific absolutism. A substantial difference in commitment arises on the score of justification of methods of scientific inquiry. From both the pragmatic and the realist standpoints the feasibility of what I have called 'surface justification', that is, the demonstration of reliability by calibration against precedents and standards, is surely crucial for the defence of scientific absolutism. But with regard to the feasibility of programmes for 'deep justification'—causal explanation of the reliabilities of scientific methods—the pragmatic and realist positions diverge sharply. From the pragmatic standpoint such programmes are surely to be welcomed for the support they may one day give to scientific absolutism; but should such programmes prove infeasible scientific absolutism would not be seriously undermined. From the realist standpoint, however, infeasibility of deep justification of scientific methods would render accumulation of truth through scientific inquiry a miracle.

Where the realist defender of scientific absolutism incurs deeper epistemological commitments than does the pragmatic defender, the boot is on the other foot when we turn to the historiography of science. Again there is some common ground. From both the pragmatic and the realist metaphysical standpoints it is incumbent on the defender of scientific absolutism to exhibit in the history of science successive approximation of past theories to our own; and it must further be shown that parts of past theories that are, by our lights, well confirmed are also typically at least approximately true from the standpoint of our theories. But as we have seen the pragmatic defender needs far more than this. Successive recognition and overcoming of sources of error, domination of other traditions of inquiry by traditions of inquiry ancestral to our science, concurrence in beliefs based on disparate bodies of evidence—these are but a sample of the processes whose prevalence in the history of science has to be substantiated.

One further divergence in commitment deserves mention. It concerns the resources drawn on in resisting radical scepticism. From the standpoint of our pragmatic account of truth the possibility that the radical sceptic envisages, that all our beliefs about the world are false, is not a genuine possibility. For on the pragmatic account it is tantamount to the supposition that there could be an interpretive standpoint from which all our beliefs about the world came out false under an adequate interpretation scheme. At the end of Chapter V a well-known argument for the impossibility of that supposition was endorsed. From the realist metaphysical standpoint this rebuttal of radical scepticism is unavailable. However, it would be premature for a pragmatic defender of scientific absolutism to see in this divergence a straightforward victory for pragmatism. To be sure the onus is on the metaphysical realist to refute the standard arguments for radical scepticism. But possession of an argument for the impossibility of the radical sceptical conclusion does not exonerate the pragmatist from the daunting task of showing precisely how the long-standing seductive arguments for the impossible conclusion go wrong.[1]

Of the many large questions raised but unanswered in our defence of scientific absolutism two deserve special mention: the question of the defensibility of absolutism in fields of inquiry other that the natural sciences; and the question of the modes of accumulation of truth in the sciences.

Our defence of scientific absolutism has depended at many stages on supposed truths drawn from disciplines that manifestly are not natural sciences. For example, we have repeatedly invoked hypotheses about the history of science; the argument has depended at a number of crucial points on principles drawn from the theory of interpretation; and our pragmatic account of truth is a metaphysical account. Is absolutism in these fields defensible? If not, how can it be legitimate to appeal to them in this way?

The pragmatic account of truth does not decisively rule out the attainability of truth in a wide range of non-scientific disciplines as do realist accounts of truth as correspondence to a mind-independent world. Great difficulties, however, beset the transposition to other disciplines of the arguments for scientific absolutism presented here. Consider, for example, two of the aspects of the history of science central to our case: transcendence of error and domination of other traditions of inquiry by traditions ancestral to our science. It is hard indeed to detect analogues of these in the histories of, say, metaphysics or hermeneutic theory.[2] Further, problems of commensurability and indeterminacy of interpretation raise grave difficulties of principle for the application of such notions to the histories of these disciplines.

In considering the extension of absolutism beyond the natural sciences it may be a mistake to treat the problem as one of defending distinct brands of absolutism: metaphysical absolutism, mathematical absolutism, hermeneutic absolutism, etc. Rather, I suggest, the task should be seen as that of defending absolutism with respect to a total body of 'science' that includes beliefs from the whole range of disciplines. This Quinean position is one that has been implicitly adopted at various points in the present work; it is, for example, implicit in our treatment of alleged metaphysical *insolubilia* as direct challenges to the hypothesis that there are no specific limits to

---

[1] Cf. B. Stroud, *The Significance of Philosophical Scepticism*, Oxford, 1984, ch. 7.
[2] This point was impressed on me by Mary Hesse.

scientific inquiry. Further, our attempt to ground scientific absolutism in the history of science and our proposals about the modes of establishment of the reliability of scientific methods may be seen as modest exercises in Quinean naturalization. The types of naturalization essayed in this work are, however, surely insufficient to validate a Quinean notion of total science. It would be a major undertaking to survey the various ways in which substantive interdisciplinary connections may be established; but it is worth mentioning a couple of modes of integration that are of particular relevance to metaphysics, epistemology, and the theory of interpretation, the disciplines whose pretensions to yield truths are of most immediate concern to us. First, there is the integration that occurs when theses from one discipline are shown to have explanatory roles in another. Thus, to take an example that has already received critical mention, epistemology would be integrated with biology if a convincing evolutionary explanation of the reliability of scientific methods could be found. Integration of a second important type is brought about when critical reflection on inquiry in one discipline shows such inquiries to be grounded in activities and tacit assumptions proper to another discipline. Thus it may be argued that natural scientific inquiry, involving as it does interpretation of the scientific activities and beliefs of others, is grounded in the practice and theory of interpretation.[3]

On the question of the mode of accumulation of truth in science certain hypotheses have already been ventured. The point has been emphasized that scientific inquiries do not face a fixed agenda of questions, but that there is rather a turnover, as new theories and methods render old questions ill-posed and bring to light new ones. In Chapter II a view of scientific inquiry as open-ended was urged against the depressing image of the sequence of scientific theories as convergent upon an ultimate all-encompassing theory. It has been repeatedly suggested that accumulation of truth in science has been unsteady and piecemeal rather than steady and across the board. Further, it has been argued that though accumulation of truth in science has often occurred through intertheorretic reduction, that reduction is generally of the partial and approximative kind that displaces substantial parts of the reduced theory.

[3] This line of argument has famously been pursued by Jürgen Habermas, *Erkenntnis und Interesse* (1968), trans. J. J. Shapiro, *Knowledge and Human Interests*, Boston, 1971.

There remain, however, many further pressing and currently controversial questions. For example, though something has been said about ways in which old scientific questions may be dissolved by new theories, the far harder issue of the modes of emergence of new scientific questions has been left untackled. Nor have we tackled a whole series of questions about the disciplinary loci and theoretical levels of accumulation of truth in science. Does such accumulation occur at the level of general theory as well as at the level of empirical generalizations and experimental and 'phenomenological' laws? If accumulation occurs only or chiefly at the empirical level, how is that level to be characterized? Does the accumulation of truth in science involve unification of fields of inquiry? If so, does such unification occur primarily through interaction of fields, or is there rather a hierarchy of fields, those of higher rank tending to engulf those below them?

Our discussions of the history of science have been conducted at too high a level of generality to permit any but the most tentative remarks on such questions. They do, however, tend to cast doubt on physicalist views which claim an accumulation of truth at the level of high physical theory and treat microreduction as a primary mode of scientific progress.[4] They provide perhaps a modicum of support for Duhemian views of accumulation of truth in science as occurring largely at the level of experimental and low-level theoretical laws;[5] and they may also support an account of scientific progress that emphasizes proliferation and interaction of fields of inquiry.[6] My suspicion is, however, that a more detailed appeal to the history of science would sustain few positive generalizations; it would, rather, encourage the notion of an irreducible plurality of modes of accumulation of truth in science.

---

[4] The current prevalence of such hard-line physicalist views owes much to Wilfrid Sellars's *Science, Perception and Reality*, London, 1963, and J. J. C. Smart's *Philosophy and Scientific Realism*, London, 1963.

[5] P. Duhem, *La théorie physique, son objet et sa structure* (2nd edn., 1914), trans. P. P. Weiner, *The Aim and Structure of Physical Theory*, Princeton, 1954. Duhemian views on truth in science have been promoted by M. B. Hesse, *Revolutions and Reconstructions in the Philosophy of Science*, Brighton, 1980, ch. 6, and N. Cartwright, *How the Laws of Physics Lie*, Oxford, 1983.

[6] On progress through interaction of fields see, e.g., L. Darden and N. Maull, 'Interfield theories', *Philosophy of Science*, 44 (1977), 43–64.

Index of Names

Index of Subjects

accumulation of truth, *see* truth
alien intelligences, 18, 19, 47–51
assimilation of inquiries, 23, 48–56

bridge-laws, 65–6

calibration,
of measuring apparatus, 63, 98–100,
102
of methods of theory assessment,
103–6
categorial frameworks, 124, 132–3
Chinese science, 4, 50, 51, 53–4
concurrence of beliefs, 17, 23–4, 43,
53
confirmation, 61–2, 67–8
conservatism, principle of, 69
convergence, Cauchy, 15
of theories, 14–20
Weierstrass, 14–15
see also concurrence
correspondence principle, 69

disconfirmation, 61
domination of inquiries, 23, 28–9,
30–1, 36–7, 47–56, 78
Duhem–Quine thesis, *see*
underdetermination

empirical equivalence, 62, 80–94
see also underdetermination
epistemology, 10, 32–5, 55, 56,
95–119, 134–5
evolutionary, 109–10
genetic, 110–11
naturalized, 96, 108–11
and psychology, 108–11
see also justification, limits to
inquiry, methods, reliability,
scepticism
error, 10, 18–19, 26–7, 31, 36, 38–42,
55, 69–70
observational, 39, 41
methodological, 39–41
transcendence of, 19, 20, 26–7, 36,
39–42, 69–70
see also fallibilism, scepticism

evidence, 3, 22, 25–6, 29–30, 36, 41–4,
56, 60–3, 81–94, 123–4, 132–3
accessibility of, 29–30, 36, 41–4, 56,
81–2, 88–9
theory-dependence of, 3, 25–6,
60–3, 81
and well-posedness of questions,
25–6, 123–4, 132–3
see also empirical equivalence,
evidential compensation,
measurement
evidential compensation, 42–4
evidential equivalence, *see* empirical
equivalence
evolutionary epistemology, *see*
epistemology
explanation, 23, 27–8, 48–56, 69–70,
71, 77–8, 102–3, 112–19, 120–1,
122, 123
of divergence of inquiries, 23, 27–8,
30–1, 48–56, 69–70
and interpretation, 71, 77–8
of reliability of methods, 102–3,
109, 112–19

fallibilism, 10, 33
falsification, 61, 82

genetic epistemology, *see*
epistemology

historiography, 1–5, 24, 51–2, 91, 132,
135
holism, *see* interpretation
humanity, principle of, *see*
interpretation

incommensurability,
of theories, 9, 25, 58, 73
of styles of inquiry, 125
indeterminacy,
causal, 121
of interpretation, 9, 25, 58, 74
interpretation, 5, 9, 25, 55, 58, 70–80,
89
criteria of adequacy of, 70–9
historical, 5